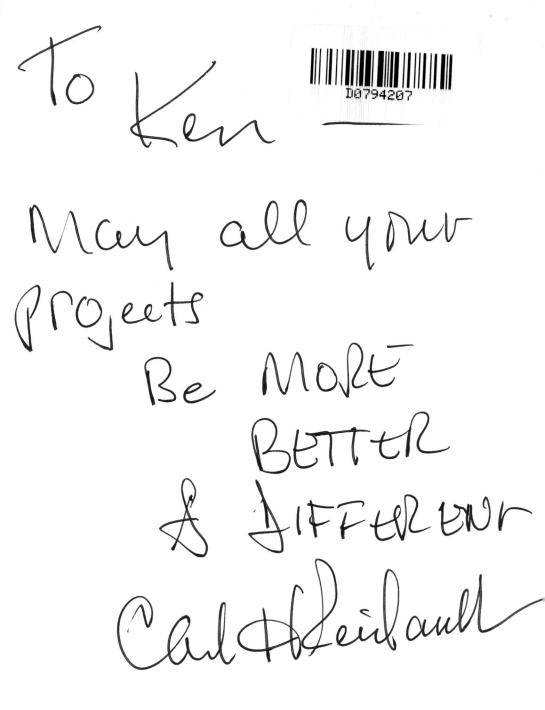

To Ken —

May all your
projects
    Be MORE
        BETTER
    & DIFFERENT

Carl Reinbandt

More, Better, Different

More, Better, Different

Getting What You Want through a Proven Dynamic for Successful Leadership

Robert W. Lauridsen, PhD, and Carl H. Reinhardt, CEO with Fran E. Lauridsen, PhD

"Highly recommended."

Burt Nanus, professor emeritus of management, University of Southern California, and author of *Visionary Leadership* and *Leaders Who Make a Difference*

MORE, BETTER, DIFFERENT
GETTING WHAT YOU WANT THROUGH A PROVEN
DYNAMIC FOR SUCCESSFUL LEADERSHIP

iUniverse books may be ordered through booksellers or by contacting:

iUniverse
1663 Liberty Drive
Bloomington, IN 47403
www.iuniverse.com
1-800-Authors (1-800-288-4677)

Because of the dynamic nature of the Internet, any web addresses or links contained in this book may have changed since publication and may no longer be valid. The views expressed in this work are solely those of the author and do not necessarily reflect the views of the publisher, and the publisher hereby disclaims any responsibility for them.

Any people depicted in stock imagery provided by Thinkstock are models, and such images are being used for illustrative purposes only. Certain stock imagery © Thinkstock.

ISBN: 978-1-5320-0309-7 (sc)
ISBN: 978-1-5320-0307-3 (hc)
ISBN: 978-1-5320-0308-0 (e)

Library of Congress Control Number: 2016911926

Print information available on the last page.

iUniverse rev. date: 11/16/2016

Praise for *More, Better, Different*

This book breaks new ground in the all-important quest to translate vision into reality. Successful execution is the key to progress in any organization, and these authors have distilled their decades of experience into a systematic, proven, and highly practical system for moving an organization to a new, higher level of accomplishment. A must read!

—Burt Nanus, professor emeritus of management, University of Southern California, author of *Visionary Leadership* and *Leaders Who Make a Difference*

More, Better, Different describes one of the most powerful, proven, people-oriented systems for developing agility and generating results ever developed.

—Mark Morgan, CEO, Stratex Partners, Inc.

Great to hear your new book is ready for publishing. You've captured the system you shared with us in your consulting. We understood our values and had a clear set of goals, a strategic direction, and an organizational design. What we needed were the skills and the tools to execute. Using your high-performance accountability system has helped our executive teams evolve into integrated, productive teams. This book will help us with our training to continuously deliver customer delight. I highly recommend it to people who have to get things done through the efforts of others.

—Tom Hayse, CEO, ETM

Carl and Bob have been meaningfully touching lives with their inspired process to help leaders and individuals take action where it matters most, for themselves. Their ability to empathically listen and meaningfully help others is now being shared for individuals to learn within the pages of *More, Better, Different*. I love that they've thoughtfully shared their ideas to potentially help millions of lives.

—Alex Potts, CEO, Loring Ward

The most impressive aspect I have garnered from the More, Better, Different System you shared with me at Oracle Corporation is not only how valuable the key elements of the training have been to my own day-to-day managerial approach, but how easily I was able to transfer these precepts to my team to immediately improve their efficiency. My team follows through on commitments in a timelier manner, and they also observe the same with their internal and external partners. In addition, satisfaction levels have increased as people better understand their roles and expectations. We'll begin using more of the concepts and tools you've detailed in *More, Better, Different,* and I can't wait to get copies of your new book for my team.

—Bill Analla, senior program manager, Bill.com

Great that you have your system in book format and can't wait to see the final version. Recently I shared with my executive associates how you and your high-performance accountability system have been keys to our success. Your system not only encourages us to work collaboratively; it insists on it. Once we learned and implemented the system, those who would not or could not work in a way that made us all better began to surface. Over time we successfully coached some to step up, and we replaced others with more committed types. We've seen the difference.

—Alain Labat, CEO, Harvest Management Partners, Inc.

Congratulations on your new book. Bob Lauridsen and Carl Reinhardt have taken sophisticated management theories and direct experience derived from many consulting engagements and direct CEO-level experience and synthesized a practical "management system" that can be transformational for teams striving to improve their operational effectiveness and delivery of results. Its foundation is built around a "committed communications" model and a strong system of accountability, two core components for building high-performance teams. This system contributed to achieving improved team alignment, accountability, and results at VaST Systems, Inc.!

—Michael Paczan, CTO and senior vice president of engineering, VaST Systems Technology, Inc., and consultant

They've captured in their new book, *More, Better, Different,* the system they helped us implement. Dr. Lauridsen and Carl Reinhardt's consulting process gave our management team the tools to move out of a state of frustration and conflict into a state of cooperation and success. Given our past success, I was eager to read their new book, *More, Better, Different.* To my delight, I found that Lauridsen and Reinhardt streamline the task of setting and achieving goals into logical, easy-to-follow steps. They also spend time coaching the reader through common challenges that might occur and how to address these challenges. Once again, I am impressed with the authors' ability to get to the heart of business breakdowns that result in failure to establish and meet goals, while educating the reader on how to create a successful path to establish and consistently achieve its goals.

—Christi Becerra, CFO, Terrapin Systems

More than a book, *better* than a book, and *different* in the most profound and profitable ways from existing books treating this subject, such is the fruit of Lauridsen's stellar twenty-five years of corporate consulting and Reinhardt's twenty-five years of growing several companies, including his financial firm with $3 billion in assets under management. I am excited to know that thanks to this text, readers all over the world will gain access to the same insights that were essential to my success. This book should, and hopefully will, be required reading for business schools or for anyone who wants to see real and dramatic improvements in life and business.

—Mike A. Dixon, MBA, CFP©, CIMC, CIMA, Dixon Financial Services, president and investment adviser

Congratulations on your new book, *More, Better, Different.* I am impressed with the simple yet powerful—and universal—nature of these concepts and tools. They create clarity around commitments and lead to getting things done. As proven techniques, they work with both functional and project teams! For anyone looking for opportunities to develop better team interactions, avoid slippage, and develop an accountability culture, this book is for you.

—Randall L. Englund, author, executive consultant, trainer, international consultant, and expert on project management

I appreciate your having sent me the prepublished version of your new book. You have expanded on the work you did with us and deepened the context of your powerful system. I can now understand more fully what we did in your training and consulting program where I was looking for two things: clarity and focus. After two months in the program, that was achieved in spades. Not only was I more focused, but my entire team was enjoying the fruits of my participation in the program. We were able to implement a new way of interacting with each other based on commitments, we finished projects that never seemed to get done, and we reached new milestones in terms of service and support. In addition to what our team and the business were able to accomplish, I personally gained an expansive collection of new communication, management, and sales tools and techniques that have made me a better manager, a better communicator, and a better leader. Thanks for publishing the system.

—Jonathan Scheid, president and chief investment officer, Bellatore Financial, Inc.

CONTENTS

ACKNOWLEDGMENTS

Few books are written without the contributions of many people. We are grateful to Fernando Flores for having identified and described a perspective and foundation for truly effective interactions, which are central to any leader's success. This book is our attempt to provide for managers a proven productivity perspective and practical tools that have been developed by combining Carl's experience as a CEO and Robert's international consulting experience.

From Robert:

Burt Nanus, professor emeritus of management, University of Southern California, and author of *Visionary Leadership* and *Leaders Who Make a Difference*, gets a special acknowledgment for his guidance and ready willingness to share his vast wisdom with me. This book stands on the shoulders of his research and international work with corporations.

I wish to thank all those leaders who listened, learned with us, and taught us, providing new ways of looking at the system we were developing. Steven J. Sherman, coauthor of my first book, *Boss Talk … A Manager's Guide to Exceptional Productivity and Innovation*, gets a special nod for bringing the productivity system into Adobe.

Special thanks go to Tom Hayse, CEO, ETM, who has implemented our concepts and tools throughout his company over a ten-year period, adding some of the tools we have shared in this book.

I'd also like to thank both Alain Labatt and Kyle Park, formerly with VaST, Inc., for sponsoring the high-performance system internationally and adding to its effectiveness.

Thanks go to Click-Away's Rick Sutherland, CEO, and Oliver Rowen, president, who have sponsored implementation of the high-performance productivity system in their company and collaborated on various refinements that have added impact to the process of teaching people a new interaction dynamic.

Thanks to Mark Morgan and Randy Englund, who helped us get clear on the value of developing and driving projects as one of the keys to corporate success. Additional thanks to Randy for allowing us to lift a large portion of the sponsorship chapter from his book.

Our editors from iUniverse and Jan Stiles have guided us on this journey, providing insight and recommendations of inestimable value. I would also like to thank Dedi Hanson for her support in getting this book produced.

Special thanks to Carl, my coauthor and friend, who—through his grasp of productivity concepts and his deep knowledge of the inner workings of business—has a unique capacity to take the system I have been developing to a new level. Most importantly I have learned firsthand from Carl that the ultimate reward is in the giving, not the receiving.

Finally, I want to thank my wife, Dr. Fran Lauridsen, for driving this collaborative effort and for being deeply involved in the development and implementation of the productivity system through her own and joint corporate consulting projects. The book would not have happened without her expertise and guidance and her collaborative efforts with Carl and me.

And from Carl:

Thanks and acknowledgment go to my mentor, Thomas F. McLaughlin, who hired me as an intern and then sat down with me and made sure that we both passed our security license in 1969. Thanks also to George Pearson, VP at Ohio National, who taught me the ropes while traveling in the South representing the Pension Department, all the while teaching me the importance of hard work and of building lasting, trustworthy relationships and friendships with clients.

To my former partners Alan Werba and John Bowen: together we realized that different individuals with different talents who have a common goal can change an industry by being a powerful team. To Alex Potts, Mike Clinton, and my sons Erich and Matthew Reinhardt, my thanks for having taught me that the younger generation has great ideas and ambition that the older generation really needs to listen to.

Thanks to my partners, Tracy Newquist and Dan Newquist. Both she and Dan helped me grow our firm along with the rest of the RNP team in Morgan Hill.

Hats off to John Burroughs, chairman of Lighthouse Bank and chairman of Foothill Securities, as well as the executive management team at Foothill Securities: Steve Chipman, the president; Mike Melby, the CFO; and Rex Gardiner, the founder. They have built and maintained a successful broker-dealer business whose representatives are actually the owners of the firm. Special thanks to Ann Marie Sheehan and Mike Destro. Their camaraderie has taught me to always give more than you receive.

A special thanks to colleagues like Mike Dixon and Rob Kemp who have been my friends through thick and thin times in the investment management profession and have shown me that true camaraderie is also mutual everlasting respect. And to Fran and Bob Lauridsen, who have shown us that goals without pathways, projects, and tasks are only wishful thinking until accountability steps in.

Thanks to my clients who are also my friends, who have entrusted me with their retirement plans, investments, and confidentiality; this responsibility I have accepted and cherish.

To my good friends George Chiala, who taught me that faith is the rock of perseverance, and Mike Beasley, who always states that the one thing we all have in common is time—my thanks for showing me that it's what we do with that time that makes us different.

Most of all, thank you to my wife and partner, Gerrie, who has always been at my side with support and encouragement. She is the mastermind of our household budget and appointments, and after forty-nine years, I can still say she is the love of my life.

INTRODUCTION

Staying Competitive in a Changing World

Have you ever wondered how effective you are as a leader of your company, department, or team? Do you have tools or methods that you use to evaluate the qualities, strategies, or processes you bring to that leadership position? If you could isolate a few key elements—ones that could help you strengthen and build your company or team into the future—would you want to learn how to use them to enhance your company and your own career?

These critical elements exist, and this book will show you how to put them to work for you.

We're referring to the ability to envision your company's potential and to recognize what needs to change in order for you to achieve your goals for the future. Such change begins with identifying what you need more of, what you need to do better, and what needs to be different about your operation. We refer to this focus, in short, as *more, better, different.*

To put more, better, different to work for your company, you need a system that helps you move effectively and consistently from ideas and desired outcomes to actual results. This system has to include practices and tools you can use to describe what you want the company to be, to set the goals that will get you there, and to develop the plan to achieve those goals. It begins with your commitment to move beyond the status quo.

Someone happy with the status quo typically doesn't hold a leadership role—at least not for the long term. To these people, everything looks fine as it is. "Why waste the effort on a future that may never materialize?" they ask. Effective leaders, however, see what's working, what's not, and what could be. They understand that the status quo can lead to complacency. They make an effort to listen and look for what might be going wrong, where there might be opportunities for improvement, and what advantages might be gained by doing something different. These leaders want more for their companies—and for themselves. They envision the desired future condition, design a path to its attainment, and set out on that path to attain their goals.

But here's the problem. According to Mark Morgan, a highly successful corporate consultant and lecturer at Stanford University, and his cowriters in the book *Executing Your Strategy*, "Business schools unleash throngs of aspiring strategists and big-picture thinkers into the corporate world every year. Yet studies have found that less than 10 percent of effectively formulated strategies carry through to successful implementation."[1]

Why does this happen?

The Challenge of Leadership

Leaders and managers responsible for producing through the efforts of those who report to them face a variety of challenges. They typically point to things like misunderstanding, misplaced self-interest, and failure to follow through. They need to know how to motivate various kinds of employees with varying agendas. They may be frustrated at having to deal with frequent breakdowns, blown handoffs, or a failure to collaborate, all of which can lead to confrontations, missed deliveries, or unhappy customers.

In some cases, companies are moving so fast that leaders are continually fighting fires and feel they have no time to step back, analyze what we call the *now* situation, develop a plan for the *future*, and then effectively implement that plan. Others fail to recognize the importance of taking the time to envision the future, or they lack the confidence to develop a strong plan that will carry them through to implementation. Some find it difficult to focus beyond day-to-day problems and breakdowns. Too often they struggle with balancing their attention between daily operational hurdles and long-term strategic direction.

We believe these leaders need a new approach. To that end, we have devoted much of our twenty-five years of coaching, consulting, and managing to the observation and examination of today's challenges and the development of practical, reliable, real-world solutions. The result is the identification of a dynamic that enables leaders to create more effective working environments, thus achieving the outcomes they envision for their companies. We believe that what we have to offer is a fresh approach, developed incrementally over time and tested against real workplace situations and challenges.

Why Traditional Approaches Are Inadequate

For decades, businesses leaders have sought solutions to behavioral and operational problems through corporate training initiatives, management-skills workshops, and how-to books. But such mediums often categorize behaviors (communicating, influencing, resolving conflict, etc.) and thus address only pieces of the problem at a time. This organizational approach makes it easier for trainers to teach new behaviors, but it also means that leaders and trainees may focus more on these individual elements and behaviors and lose sight of what the system as a whole is intended to achieve for the organization.

Programs that seek to support more long-term and sweeping changes are often large and complex, and the overall vision may be difficult to communicate clearly to frontline workers. Buy-in becomes an issue, as does the ability to keep the long-term outcome in sight while implementing the details of day-to-day process improvements. What many programs lack is a clear system of flexible yet disciplined and applicable behaviors, skills, interactions, and practices that overlay *all* corporate behavior and that weave seamlessly from the production line to the executive offices. As a result, successful change achieved in one department or on one level is not always matched by similar and parallel changes throughout the organization.

In our work advising and coaching leaders in a variety of companies, we have observed the breakdowns, blown handoffs, and failures to collaborate that frustrate leaders every day. Over the years, leaders at all levels have asked us the following questions:

- ➢ How can we keep up with the competition we're facing?
- ➢ How can I know when my strategy is not working—sooner rather than later?
- ➢ What can I do to get visibility into all my projects, initiatives, and processes without micromanaging?
- ➢ If execution is 90 percent people and 10 percent technical, how do I deal effectively with the 90 percent?
- ➢ How do I bridge the chasm between my commitments and my employees' reliability in doing the things they promise to do?

In attempting to address these concerns, we came to understand that the management paradigm from which many leaders were operating no longer served them the way it had in the past. Rather, we needed new tools and practices to address these concerns. And we needed to incorporate them into an effective management model or system for getting things done.

What We Have Learned

As our corporate consulting services moved us in and out of large, medium, and small companies, we found that most organizations experience similar issues around producing and executing goals and strategy. We learned that management science—the current accepted systems and processes that inform leaders on how to get results—has not kept up with the complexity, issues, and attitudes that leaders now face.

The nature of work today calls for new perspectives and new practices that have not always been taught or institutionalized. Over time, we began to see that if companies were to succeed and grow in this competitive, ever-changing environment, they would need to foster a successful operational dynamic of working with and through others. Their leaders would have to be exposed to a new system and would need to master new tools and develop new ways of working with and through others.

Ironically, one of the problems that we didn't see at first was that we were operating from the same broken leadership model as our clients and were therefore having difficulty delivering the results we had promised. Our inability to resolve their issues satisfactorily led to our being as frustrated as they were.

Early on in his career as a consultant, for example, author Lauridsen promised to work with a CEO's executives to help them better solve problems and improve work processes and relationships. He experienced his own breakdown, however, when several managers routinely failed to show up for their weekly coaching session, despite having committed to do so.

Frustrated, Lauridsen sat in an office at one of his client's sites trying to determine what had gone wrong and what, if anything, he could do about it. In that unforgettable moment, he understood that managers had certain kinds of powers that he did not have at his disposal. In a hierarchical system, a manager assesses and rates his or her people, influences decisions regarding pay and position, and often has the right to promote, transfer, or fire someone. Managers can make something happen by telling someone to do something, and consequences loom behind this strong request for action.

As a consultant, however, Lauridsen had no such power. There were no immediate or apparent consequences for employees' failing to respond to his requests or suggestions. In fact, he did not even have the right to make requests. Nor could he strongly encourage or demand that anyone cooperate or collaborate with him. Even so, he was charged with achieving a specific result for the organization, and that outcome required people's cooperation. Promises had been made and he was getting paid, but he couldn't get key people to meet with him.

With this realization, it dawned on him why, in previous engagements, he had not gotten the results he had intended. With that knowledge, he began to design a system that fostered cooperation and collaboration and that insisted on people supporting one another. The system also allowed him to get the support he needed in order to deliver on promises to the leader who had hired him. Finally, Lauridsen was able to bottle up the entire process, turn it into a program of skills he could deliver, and share it with leaders and managers who, he had discovered, were as frustrated as he was about not achieving intended results.

After a few similar experiences, Lauridsen and his consulting staff realized that to help clients (and themselves, as it turned out), they needed to design a teachable process that leaders could follow to set direction, establish goals, and execute on achieving those goals. The process would have to guide leaders through the effort of translating top-level concepts into understandable actions that ultimately delivered customer delight, worker satisfaction, and company profit.

Not everything the consultants tried was successful. Not all techniques worked in all environments. Yet, gradually, they found reliable methods and solutions. They began to see some tools working consistently. They observed leaders who, by employing the skills they had learned, felt empowered to diagnose problems and to apply solutions.

With lessons learned in previous failures and a sizable accumulation of observations and shared communications from clients, Lauridsen and his staff created the first versions of a high-performance productivity system that they could share with managers. Feedback from clients helped them improve the system, so that it would address today's unique leadership and managerial challenges from a new perspective. One client, Carl Reinhardt, began to see the competitive advantage of the system being applied at his company and suggested collaborating on a book. The result is this blend of Lauridsen's twenty-five years of corporate consulting experience and Reinhardt's twenty-five years of leading several companies, including taking his financial firm to $2.5 billion in assets under management, with the help of his partners.

Author Reinhardt is himself no stranger to the perils of the status quo. Having reached the top of his field with his firm of financial advisers, he understands that change often gives rise to feelings of vulnerability that not only hit leaders on the inside as worry and insecurity but also pose real threats to a company's continued viability and success. Reinhardt experienced this twice in his own management career. The first occurred when his firm switched from commission payouts to fee generation, a change that caused him and his partners to endure two years without income. A second period of no income followed his decision to leave his position as a top executive in order to start an investment planning firm with his wife as his only employee. To keep their business viable, neither of them drew a salary until they secured an established clientele.

Through both of these experiences, Reinhardt found that staying focused on the purpose behind the change and on the desire for a new now was critical in developing and implementing an effective plan for the future. He realized that leaders who want— or need—to change their now situation have to first inventory the present situation and then start the commitment process to analyze where they want to be in the future. Once they set the direction, they need the passion to keep going, knowing and believing that the future will ultimately become a new and better now. For Reinhardt, putting together teams of capable and creative people, working in alignment with everyone, and moving toward the envisioned future with integration and accountability have played critical roles in keeping his firm in positive territory and at the top of its field.

Similarly, the productivity system that had its beginning in Lauridsen's earlier work has proved its value for leaders again and again. With each application, the authors have made new observations and polished their approach, learning more about how well the overall elements adapt to the specific needs and goals of each company that implements them. Their purpose in writing this book is to share with you a proven system of leadership for those working in the role of producer. Recognizing and understanding the critical but often overlooked role of leader as producer, or the executor of strategy, is where this book begins.

How to Increase Control over Intended Outcomes

Consider that the professional outcomes you are getting now are appropriate to the system you have in place and to the systems that may exist in your environment. Our purpose in writing this book is to show you how to increase your control over those outcomes. The more, better, different system offers a new perspective on how work gets done and thereby optimizes the odds that what you intend to accomplish will actually happen. In that sense, it is about power. Not the kind of power associated with domination, but the power of getting done what you say you will get done through the contributions of others.

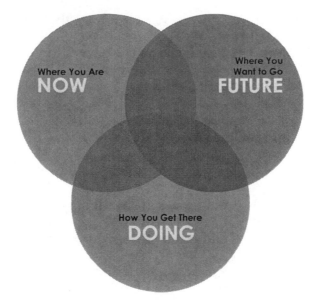

The system's three key elements are as follows:

1. **Now** (Circle 1)

   Your journey begins with an objective reality check of the present or now situation for your business or for you as a leader in an organization. After you have determined the present situation of your business or of yourself as an owner or leader, we'll guide you into circle 2, which we call the *future*.

2. **The Future** (Circle 2)

   In circle 2 you begin addressing your desired future by determining what you really intend to accomplish. You learn a simple, proven methodology that positions you for action. Then we focus on the generation of results that happens in circle 3, the *doing*.

3. **The Doing** (Circle 3)

   Finally, in circle 3 you have a methodology of doing (taking action) that provides a step-by-step system for moving things forward and getting things done, whether you work alone or must depend on others for the execution of tasks and assignments.

You can use this three-circle process throughout your career to continuously assess, update, and fine-tune your business or your career as a leader. The process also helps you stay in alignment with your own and your customers' and clients' intentions and expectations.

The more, better, different system is simple and transformational. It is not a disconnected set of tips and advice, but rather a complete, proven system for increasing strategy-focused productivity and innovation. Over time, we followed star leaders, observing their interactions (conversations and other actions). We found that while they were successful in transforming their strategy into results, they often could not tell us what they were doing. Since they were unable to articulate their productivity system, they were largely unable to convey or cascade their competence to others who, as a result, remained less competent and often distinctly annoying to the top leaders.

Our intention here is to share the system we've developed and to demonstrate how it instills a highly productive "interaction dynamic" that shapes the way people interact with other individuals, groups, or departments for the sake of producing their products and services. This system will enable you to accomplish, consistently and reliably, the things you need to get done. To demonstrate the effect and benefits of this dynamic, we will delve into each of the elements of our strategy-focused, high-performance commitment system. You will begin to see how the complementary nature of the system's elements acts to leverage the effectiveness of its tools and methods. You will find here a system and specific steps you can use to

1. set clear goals that your people agree to and stick with;
2. set up an environment that fosters collaboration and accountability;

3. reliably identify what works and what doesn't in a snap;

4. know what to do with breakdowns in delivery—right now; and

5. know how to take care of your own as well as your people's satisfaction and vitality in the process.

By the end of this book, you will understand how the system provides both an individual and a corporate competitive advantage. You will see how it can impact your present and future success.

How to Read This Book

This book is divided into three sections, as follows:

1. Determining the present situation—your now—and identifying both opportunities and weak points for improvement

2. Planning a strategy that leads to actionable projects intended to produce desired outcomes—your future

3. Getting those projects done—the doing

A truly good leader can never know too much about what goes into determining the most effective means for setting and implementing goals. Although we know this, we had serious concerns that the now and future sections of the book—which address transforming ideas and goals for the future into projects— would be viewed as being out of touch with our audience and perhaps overly simplified. After all, everyone knows about goals and projects. Why would anyone read that stuff?

Yet as we traveled the country and worked with all levels of leaders, we repeatedly encountered situations in which leaders did indeed *know* the terminology but were not, in fact, creating clear goals and projects that focused people's energy and gained their commitment. Interestingly, those leaders with higher levels of experience and knowledge actually became our strongest advocates for revisiting the goal-setting portion of the system.

That said, welcome to the more, better, different leadership system. Let's get started.

In chapter 1 you will learn about some of the enemies to success and describe situations that can stop your productivity and/or change effort. Armed with a knowledge of these enemies, you will begin to see how you can optimize the odds that what you intend to accomplish will actually get done.

PART 1

From Now to the Future

CHAPTER 1

Working in and Working on the Business

There are times when you are working toward a goal and your current productivity system is working. You may, however, begin to see that your system for getting things done is not good enough. Consider that whenever you entertain new ideas about how things could be better, you are considering some form of change. The current status is not good enough, so you are looking to change something. Regarding change, a critical distinction for your success in business is knowing when you are working *in* the business and when you are working *on* the business. You know you are working *in* the business when you're doing the day-to-day tasks and activities, the stuff that just keeps coming at you, such as

> things you promised,
>
> calls you need to make,

reports you have to complete,

projects you're working on, and

meetings you need to attend.

Isn't it true that these go on and on throughout the day? When we are doing these things, we claim that we are working *in* the business. We are carrying out day-to-day activities by doing the tasks and delivering on the commitments that make up our business and that produce our income. We could say that the day-to-day stuff is living in the foreground of our awareness; thus, we typically attend to it. If we're diligent, we get things done.

We are okay with this for some period of time, but ideas are buzzing in the background that need to be addressed. These ideas are on the back burner and might include considering increasing sales, opening a new office, working fewer hours, or having someone take over some of your responsibilities. You also might be thinking about having more customers, more income, better ways of getting new clients, or a different way of working with associates and clients. Consider that what is running around in the background is your mind churning through what we call your more, better, and different (MBD) list. These could also be called the wants and desires that live as thoughts or ideas—or even

dreams for your future. The key point here is that in this moment these MBDs live *only* as ideas, yet they are precursors to deciding to go into action. When you go into action addressing one of these items, we say you are now working *on* the business, rather than *in* it.

From Ideas to Action

So how do you move ideas from the background into the foreground so that you can begin to see these items more clearly? In other words, how do you begin to get clear on those items you might want to take some action on, rather than have them buzzing around creating anxiety and down moods because you just never get going on any of them? As a first step, you can simply list them, so that now they are living in a documented form, rather than just as background ideas. Sounds simple, and it is. But how often do we take the time to document our ideas? Once you have documented or listed your ideas, you are on your way. However, at this point, good, hardworking people typically roll up their sleeves and get to work on the items, overlooking a key step.

A.   B.

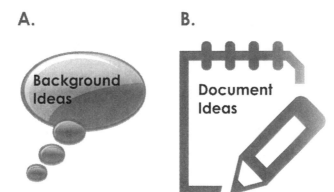

We have found that the next step, prioritizing your documented items, is often overlooked. The big difference between working in the business and working on the business is that when you are working on the business it is difficult to make a priority, because it doesn't seem crucial to the business's ability to run smoothly, whereas the mundane stuff always does. When you don't prioritize according to the importance of each idea, you then live in what we call *ideas land*, a place in the mind where all ideas are good ideas and everything gets addressed, often leading to a shortage of resources, frustration, and breakdown.

The problem with ideas land is that not all ideas are good ideas, and as a result, this becomes the land of no action where nothing gets done.

Consider that if you don't prioritize, you are committing the sin of thinking you can do everything that's on your mind at any given moment. In our organizational therapy jargon, this is a *cognitive distortion*, another way of saying that your thinking is messed up. Good luck!

Steve Jobs allegedly said, "People think focus means saying yes to the things you've got to focus on. But that's not what it means at all. It means saying no to the hundred other good ideas."[1]

If you have taken our advice and prioritized—congratulations, you are now ready to take action on your first item.

But wait … something is afoot.

It turns out that there is a good reason you don't take action on these items by addressing them. Why is that? Because the very moment you address even one of your ideas and decide to go into action, you're unwittingly shifting out of working *in* the business to now working *on* the business. In other words, you're considering, without realizing it, adding extra work to your already too-busy schedule.

We know all of you have more than enough to do without adding one more action item. A perfect example of this in another area of your life is deciding to remodel your kitchen or your entire house. You may not realize at the time you decide to take on this new project that *none of your other responsibilities will have magically disappeared.* Shortly, however, the realization of what this new project means to your time and energy becomes painfully apparent. Talk to people who have just had their first child. Often what happens here is that all the things that seemed important— dishes, cleaning, errands—fall by the wayside, and they end up very disorganized as a result, because getting used to caring for the child takes over all of their focus.

The other thing you need to know is that the human mind, relatively speaking, only takes a nanosecond and little energy to think of something new to do but eons and loads of energy to do it. This reminds us of the guy who, in response to his CEO coming up with yet another project, said, "Anything can be done by the guy who doesn't have to do it." Later on you will see that there is a way to deal with this when you fill in the energy/resources section of your project template we'll provide. But we're getting ahead of ourselves.

Let's say that despite all this, you decide to address one of your ideas with the intention of shifting from ideas land into *action and results*. You're ready to go and full of energy, but danger lurks in the form of what we call enemies or barriers to taking effective action to achieve your intended result.

Enemies to Taking Action

Enemy Number One: More Work

As we noted above, when you desire things such as more money, more clients, better office work, and so forth, and you go into action, you've added a project for which you have no time—one that will require working outside of your demanding daily routine. In fact, you're now working *on* the business, and what's worse, you won't make any money by working on the business that particular day. As author Reinhardt noticed, "I'm doing all this stuff, and I'm not going to bill anybody for this. Bummer." That reality makes it very easy to get snapped back into the *real work* at hand. Working *on* the business doesn't pay immediately and just doesn't feel like real work. This can lead to a loss of energy and motivation.

Enemy Number Two: The Distraction Factor

We've found in our own experience that enemy number two, the distraction factor, lives invisibly in the background of our day-to-day work. Essentially, this is the strong possibility that we will focus on the wrong activities.

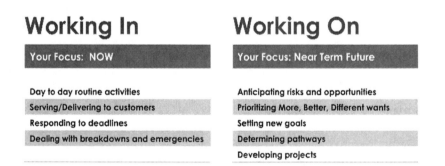

Working In
Your Focus: NOW

Day to day routine activities
Serving/Delivering to customers
Responding to deadlines
Dealing with breakdowns and emergencies

Working On
Your Focus: Near Term Future

Anticipating risks and opportunities
Prioritizing More, Better, Different wants
Setting new goals
Determining pathways
Developing projects

Day to day, we're working in the left quadrant of the "Working in and Working on" graphic shown—working in the business, managing projects, and driving all the common, day-to-day activities. We're serving our customers, responding to deadlines, and of course dealing with breakdowns with technology and/or human activities. Typically that's where we're focusing our attention and energy on a daily basis.

Once you have decided you need to work on an idea, generating something new, you have moved into the right-hand box called "Working on the Business."

When you are working *on* the business with a new project or initiative, you can easily get pulled into what feels like *the real work* in the left-hand box. This typically feels urgent and can create tension, so you may stop working on the business. Another form of distraction that doesn't feel urgent but takes us out of the working on the business mode includes various escapist activities like browsing through e-mails, researching or checking a word or concept via Google, and then going off into Google land where you completely lose focus.

It turns out that the distraction factor is a real dilemma we all face. What shall we attend to in this moment? Most important, you need to be aware of the activities and things that can pull your attention away from some intended new venture. Then, armed with awareness, you can decide how and where you will spend your precious resources of time, money, and energy. You can begin to design your focus and actions.

Enemy Number Three: Drift versus Design

This enemy is our tendency to drift along in our work, ignoring the future represented in the "Working on the Business" box.

Rather than allocating some time to look ahead and design our future, we fail to realize the value of dealing with the future, especially when it's not immediately rewarding to do so.

We say this is *drifting*, because customers' wants and needs change rapidly. Old visions and what was critical to past success that has become habitual becomes the enemy to survival. "I don't know where I'm going, but I'm headed in this direction" perfectly describes the drift.

We've now looked at three enemies to successfully getting into action and securing results. Now let's turn to enemy number four. Enemy Number Four: The absence of a system for upgrading your business by consistently translating your ideas and wants into results.

Once you have considered addressing an idea, you need a system for moving from now, to the future, to the doing. This is what we will be sharing with you in the next chapters. Our purpose is to have you be able to routinely and consistently be competent in taking your wants from the now to the future and then into effective action, the doing.

Now you have a beginning awareness of what can stop you and lead to frustration and loss of energy without your knowing it.

In our work with countless businesses, we've observed that there are really only three types of business people:

1. Those who know what to do and *do* it. They are successful, energized, satisfied, and moving forward with their business.

2. Those who know what to do and *don't* do it. These people are typically angry, frustrated, and blame others and various situations for their lack of progress.

3. Those who don't know what to do, but do something— anything. These actions can be futile or even destructive at times. The third type of business leader typically lives in hope, ignorance, and despair.

As painful as it might be, one of the best things you can do right now is to determine which of the three leaders you are at this very moment. Trust us—ignorance is not bliss. Author Reinhardt notes, "What I didn't know when I started my business was that I would, unwittingly, drift toward becoming one of these three kinds of entrepreneurs. More accurately, I was probably drifting toward some mixture of the three. Sometimes I was doing the right stuff, sometimes I was not, and sometimes I didn't know what to do—so I just did something. One problem with not knowing what to do with the consulting business was getting very busy with current clients and failing to pay attention to developing new business. Not having developed an effective system to encourage paying attention to marketing along with delivering to current clients led to slow periods with a reduced revenue stream."

Typically, no one tells us what path we're on or where we're going on that path. There is no flag, warning buzzer, or backup beeper like those installed on many trucks and cars. We're just moving along, going somewhere. The following quote woke us up one day: "If we don't change our direction, we're likely to end up where we're headed."[2]

Whether business owners or managers, most of us are definitely on a path driven by one of the three types, but will that path get us where we want to go? We've worked in the two unproductive modes, and as we mentioned, there was nothing that let us know we were in trouble. We just kept working, hoping things would work out. This discussion reminds us of Jack Kornfield's statement: "This life is a test, only a test. If it had been an actual life, you would have received further instructions on where to go and what to do."[3]

But we didn't get the instructions, so we just started doing stuff as business owners and leaders of organizations, right?

So let's get you on the right path, starting with one of your key ideas or wants and taking it into the future.

Summary

We offered the critical distinction between working *in* the business (doing the daily stuff) and working *on* the business. You know you are working in the business when you're doing the day-to-day tasks and activities, the stuff that just keeps coming at you. On the other hand, when you want more, better, or different for your company, you will be considering some form of change. You are working on the business addressing some desire and going into action doing something new. This is an important distinction for you and your people, as new projects tend to go to the back burner with day-to-day pressures insisting on your working in the business.

Then we discussed going from ideas to action, sharing the following enemies to action and success:

more work

the distraction factor

drift versus design

failing to have a system for upgrading your business
by consistently translating your MBDs into results

Next we'll jump into the key elements of your success foundation.

CHAPTER 2

Your *Now* Situation

We've all seen or read Charles Dickens's *A Christmas Carol*, where the ghosts of Christmas Present, Christmas Past, and Christmas Yet to Come visit Ebenezer Scrooge. The future is so shocking that Scrooge changes the present. In our story, we are going to help you select the future you want by *analyzing* and really *knowing* your present—the now situation.

Any GPS system can help you get to a destination, and in that way GPS has changed the mapping industry. Yet no GPS can direct you to where you want to go without first knowing where you are now.

Whether you are the owner of a business or a leader or manager working inside an organization, change is inevitable. Consider that in order to make any change, you will need to take an inventory pinpointing your current situation. With this is mind, we want to help you get what you want by again showing you the three key elements of our Foundation for Success, including

1. now—where you are now,

2. future—where you intend to go, and

3. doing—how will you get there.

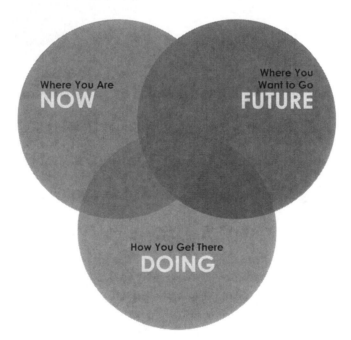

We found these three steps to be innate parts of a winning leader's repertoire.

You will soon be diving into the development of your success foundation, which will take you from your now to the future and to doing, as noted in the figure above. To start, we need to get absolutely clear as to where your business or leadership career is right now, so we will focus on circle 1. We all know our auto GPS system will get us where we want to go, but first it has to know where we are. Then and only then can it guide us to some future destination. In a similar fashion, we're creating a GPS system for you and your business by starting with your current situation.

Your Now Exercise

Let's take a look at your business or career in the simplest of all terms, using the following questions:

- What do I make and what do I spend?
- What am I earning, what is my worth on the market, or what is my business worth?
- What service or products do I sell?
- Who are my current customers, and where are the prospects for the future?
- What marketing systems are working and what systems or methods are not? Am I the only rainmaker?
- What is the current organizational chart, and is it appropriate for our future?
- Who are my affiliates or partners with whom I have business relationships?

- How often do I take time for planning, accounting, or reflecting?

- What's going well and where could there be improvements?

- What am I worth?

To focus your thinking about your now, review the items both above and below the line in the listing that follows. Then, with both feet on the ground and a clear mind, take a hard look. List *everything*; load your GPS. In our experience most leaders do not take sufficient time for this, the most important step you can take before your journey begins.

Do a quick check of expenses and income. Above the line you are looking at all of your income sources, while below the line you list all of your expenses, as follows:

Income

    Salary

    Bonus (cash stock)

    Commissions

    Fees

    Reciprocals

    Other income sources (identify each)

Expenses

> Salaries paid to employees
>
> Rent
>
> Phone
>
> Utilities
>
> Office supplies
>
> Auto/gas/insurance
>
> Marketing/advertising
>
> Business promotions
>
> Education
>
> Travel
>
> Other expenses (identify each)

Now that you've taken a first look, it's time for you to answer the questions for your current situation appropriate to your level 1 (executives) or level 2 (business owners).

Level 1: Executives, leaders, managers working inside of a business.

Questions to Prime the Pump

What is my position in the company and what role do I play?

_____

_____

_____

_____

What is the current organizational chart and is it appropriate for my future?

_____

_____

_____

_____

Regarding my career, where do I want to be in the future?

_____

_____

_____

_____

What am I earning, and what is my worth on the market? (For earning, include salary, stock, bonus, and commissions.)

_____

_____

_____

_____

Who are my associates, affiliates, or partners with whom I have business relationships?

_____

_____

_____

_____

How often do I take time for planning or assessing where I am now?

_____

_____

_____

_____

What's going well and where could there be improvements?

_____

_____

_____

_____

Is the culture of the company conducive to achieving my objectives and goals with satisfaction?

_____

_____

_____

_____

What am I worth? (Personal assets minus personal liabilities equals net worth.)

_____

_____

_____

_____

Level 2: Owners of professional businesses with one to ten employees such as consultants, real estate agents, financial advisers, physicians, and brokers

Questions to Prime the Pump

What service or products do I provide?

_____

_____

_____

_____

Who are my current customers and where are the prospects for the future?

_____

_____

_____

_____

What am I earning and what is my business worth?

_____

_____

_____

_____

What marketing systems are working and what systems are not?

_____

_____

_____

_____

Who brings in business? Who are the rainmakers?

_____

_____

_____

_____

Are expenses in line with revenue? Am I increasing my net worth?

_____

_____

_____

_____

Is my purpose conducive to achieving my goals with satisfaction and profit?

_____

_____

_____

_____

Other: Are there any other concerns regarding my now situation?

_____

_____

_____

_____

Congratulations! While these questions are not exhaustive, now that you have done the exercise, you should have a clearer understanding of your now situation. At this point, you are beginning to document what is working, what is not working, and what needs to be addressed.

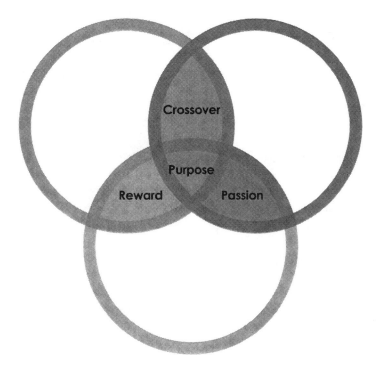

Referring to the figure above, you will notice the three overlapping areas, *crossover, passion,* and *reward.* These are connectors, and you can think of each as a blade in a propeller not only to keep you involved and motivated but to propel you forward. In the center you'll notice *purpose,* which can be thought of as the engine that drives all of your work. We like to say that your purpose drives the propellers to take your business to the sweet spot where your business is humming. Your present, future, and the doing are all aligned with your purpose. These are the psychological aspects of any change project. We claim they are often overlooked.

Before we continue with your now let's take a quick look at these areas so you can see more clearly how the process of moving from the now to the future and then to doing works.

Crossover: Once you know where you are and are looking forward to where you want to be, the exercise becomes more meaningful to activate change. Therefore, crossover becomes the first psychological mechanism of change.

Passion and Motivation: Passion creates that deep, burning desire to do what is exciting so that you become so enthusiastic that you want to step on a mountaintop and tell the world with a loud voice what you are doing. The future happens anyway in time, however, with passion you are motivated to bring about the future in line with your vision.

Reward: The reward is not just about receiving but also about giving. Once you realize that giving brings back reward tenfold, you are on the right path of reward and then the now becomes the future to always enjoy.

Purpose: Purpose can be considered your moral DNA. Purpose will include a deeply felt awareness of yourself and your calling: what the world might be asking you to do. It's everything you are, everything you've experienced, and everything you believe comprises your purpose. When you are *on purpose*, motivation is not an issue.

Sweet Spot: When you know your purpose, have studied your now, determined your desired future, and are into the doing, you are in the sweet spot, where everything is aligned. Our goal is to have everyone feel the joy of crossing over with passion and giving so that life is lived in the sweet spot.

Let's now go a bit deeper into these critical elements.

Crossover

Now that you see the process, let's return to crossover. Once you realize your now needs to change, you are ready to create your future by formulating your wants and desires. Now you are ready to cross over from the now circle to the future circle to make your business and life better.

We have found that a great tool for getting clearer on what you desire is creating your more, better, and different list or MBDs for short. The key point here is that in this moment, these MBDs live *only* as ideas yet are a precursor to deciding to go into action. When you go into action addressing one of these items, we say you are now working *on* the business, rather than *in* the business.

Prompted by the answers you gave to your now situation, please take a moment and jot down on the form below whatever more, better, or different thoughts or goals come to mind.

More (identifying what you want or need more of)

_____

_____

_____

_____

Better (noting what you need to do better or have be better)

_____

_____

_____

_____

Different (what needs to be different about your operation)

_____

_____

_____

_____

Before we go on, is there anything else you or any associates can think of regarding more, better, or different?

_____

_____

_____

_____

When you're satisfied with your list, use a pencil and prioritize all of your more, better, and different items by writing a number next to each.

Great. You are on your way.

Summary

In this chapter we've begun to address

- where you are now with your business or leadership career;
- what you would like to have more of, be better at, or change to something different; and
- prioritizing your more, better, and different items.

At this point you should have a clearer understanding of your now situation in the sense of what you want to have more of, be better at or have be better, or change to something different. You are beginning to see what is working and what is not working. You have created a MBD list and prioritized your MBDs. In the next chapter we will be taking your MBDs from crossover into the future circle by transforming them into goals.

CHAPTER 3

MBDs into the Future: From Ideas to Goals

Now that you've documented your MBDs and prioritized them, you are crossing over into the future circle with your number one MBD. Our first step is to turn that MBD into a goal—to give it an actionable format. Our purpose here is to show you how to take an idea (an MBD) and ultimately transform it into a project ready for doing.

In the next figure you can see the process of first turning your MBD into a goal, then laying out a way to achieve the goal (which we call a pathway), and then developing a project that takes you into the act of doing.

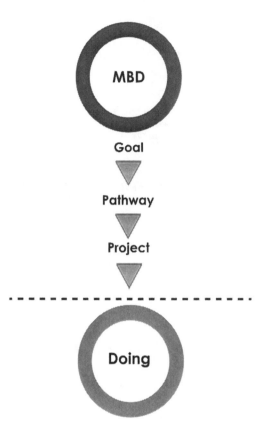

By the way, we have found in our consulting that each step in the road map is critical and that when a step that precedes another step is not handled effectively, the whole system suffers from that point on. So, for example, if your MBD is not documented and then formatted as a clear goal, the rest of the system will be off track. It really doesn't matter what you do from that point on down through the model, because you're already set up for disaster.

Author Lauridsen recalls the time he had a computer expert come to his office, and the first thing she did was check the power cord. He chuckled, but she told him he would be surprised how many times she found the cord unplugged. She clearly had a series of steps ready on hand to begin her work on people's computers. While we admit this is a weak metaphor, we'd like you to think of each step as a sort of power cord needed to address the next step in the road map.

Let's use one key MBD from one of our clients as an example to show the process just discussed.

Bill, a cofounder of a financial advisory business, wanted to increase his assets under management. He called this one of his most important mores because it would, of course, increase his income. Bill wrote his number one MBD on line one of the template shown on the next page. As noted, his MBD was a more, which he had written as "Increase assets under management." This lived only as an idea until he turned it into a goal by writing it in the *what-by-when* format: "Increase assets under management by $20 million by year-end."

MBD Worksheet

More	Better	Different	Goal
1. Increase assets under management			Increase assets by $20 million by year-end
2.	Better results from e-mail campaign		Increase campaign results by 50% by year-end
3.		Different types of clients	Increase 401(k) clients by 35%
4.			
5.			

Notice that MBDs don't typically or automatically show up as actionable goals. They are not in an actionable format because they are missing the what-by-when format that Bill used in the example above under goal.

In the template below, begin to list your more, better, or different wants. Fill in only one item for each number. If you have a more, place that in the number one slot. If you then have a different, write that in line two, and so forth.

MBD Worksheet

	More	Better	Different	Goal
1.				
2.				
3.				
4.				
5.				

Congratulations, you now have several MBDs listed on the template. You are ready to transform them into goals.

Now, referring to the template above, please take your first MBD, which is written on line one, and write a what-by-when statement for it in the goal box to the right. If, for example, you want more and your MBD is to earn more income, you would write in the goal box something to this effect: "Earn $25,000 more income by the end of this year." Now you have turned the more idea into an actionable goal. Please continue doing the same thing with each of your MBDs.

Great. You now have several MBDs written in goal format. Consider that goals are one of the most important tools for creating an extraordinary career and business. But, as you surely know by now, it takes more than simply creating goals to achieve success in any endeavor. An actionable goal without a proven system for achieving it soon turns into frustration, anger, regret, and loss of energy.

Dan Sullivan, in *The Strategic Goal Tracker*, notes, "The most successful and satisfied people are those who can imagine a bigger future and make it happen. They have the ability to set goals and achieve them. Just being able to articulate your goals is an extraordinary skill most people never develop.[1]

Summary

In this chapter we've crossed over into the future circle with your number one MBD by turning it into a goal—to give it an actionable format. In the process you have crossed over from the now circle to the future circle, where you are preparing for action. It turns out this is the first reality check into whether or not you and/or your company have the resources, energy, and time to accomplish each goal or might, in fact, be overreaching. The pathway discussion naturally leads to projects, the second reality check, which is discussed in our next chapter, where we will take the next step in developing a project.

PART 2

Between the Future
and the Doing

CHAPTER 4

Developing Pathways

Now that you have turned some MBDs into goals, it's time to determine how you will accomplish each goal.

We are using the term *pathway* to denote the process of devising ways to achieve your goals. If you think about it for a moment, once you have a goal, any goal, your next thought is probably, "How am I going to do this?" Recognized or not, the thought, *How do I do this?* is a critical precursor to other action. We call this process a *finding a pathway conversation.*

Bill began to see that the pathway discussion acted as the first reality check into whether or not the company had the resources, energy, and time to accomplish each goal or if it would instead be overreaching. The pathway discussion naturally leads to projects, the second reality check, which is discussed in our next chapter.

In conversations where effective people are interacting, we observe that they are discussing goals, pathways, and projects interchangeably. That is, they move from one notion to the next until they have pinned down how they will get a goal manifested and how they will know what they have accomplished. The very process of talking about goals, pathways, and project, begins to help clarify each element. In the process, each gets defined and refined. And since all parties participate in this collaborative effort, everyone develops a sense of agreement and ownership that is clearly missing in less effective leadership interactions.

Less effective leaders and managers seem unable to connect the three areas of goal, pathway, and project in a way that leads to specific action: that is, projects defined and agreed upon by the parties involved. Bill was an example of this kind of leader, often failing to develop a clear path to achieving a goal everyone had agreed was critical to success in the next year. Without a clear path, his people had to determine on their own how they would achieve a given goal. This resulted in misalignment, confusion, and a major breakdown in delivery.

Even worse, Bill had no awareness that his lack of understanding was leading to a breakdown. He became annoyed when consultants mentioned this to him and adroitly defended his ignorance. To his credit, a bit later he began to see where he had been missing key steps in the entire process that leads to doing. He began to own problems, rather than blame others for many of the previous year's breakdowns and disappointments. Bill later noted, "Blaming others for their stupidity kept me feeling okay about myself but sure didn't lead to the kind of results I know we can achieve." This, of course, was music to our ears. To his credit, Bill began to consult with his own employees to gather suggestions on how to achieve his goals.

While some might argue that including employees in the process of setting pathways might be inefficient, we have found the time spent doing this is a form of insurance for ensuring success. In this case, people left the meeting feeling energized and ready to meet again to further develop the project.

The step of determining pathways became, in Bill's words, "invaluable for beginning the process of resource allocation and driving us into a project. I began to see that my leadership role called for helping the team to prioritize and determine which projects we could do." As Bill had learned, exploring and determining a pathway for each goal naturally leads to the development of one or more projects, the subject of our next chapter.

Now you can use the following worksheet to write down your MBD and goals and then come up with and jot down several possible pathways.

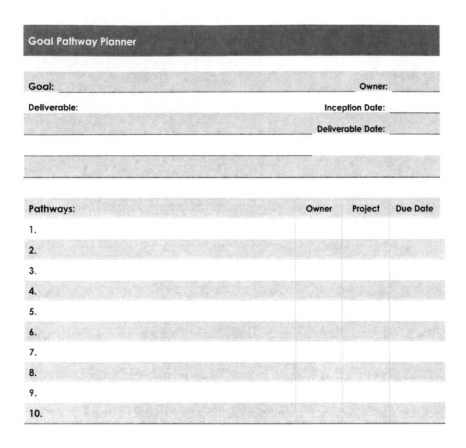

Summary

In this chapter we explored the process for determining how you will accomplish your goal, a critical precursor to taking action. We call this process a "finding a pathway conversation." We noted that the very process of talking about goals, pathways, and project begins to help clarify each element. Since each member of the group participates in this collaborative effort, a sense of alignment and ownership can be developed.

Now, armed with your pathway(s), you are ready to develop your project.

CHAPTER 5

Pathways to Projects

You've determined your goal or several goals for the year and also decided on pathways to achieving those goals. Remember—the pathway is *how* you are going to accomplish the goal. It can also be called a strategy, but we have found people like the term *pathway* because it is more precise in the context of this model.

Not only do very smart leaders often fail to discuss pathways, but they fail to take the next critical step. We can't tell you how many times groups have had, in our opinion, good conversations that included declaring goals and determining pathways to achieve the goal, but have then failed to document the discussion points and forgotten to generate a project—or just fallen asleep at the wheel. When nothing happens or progress is slow, everyone becomes frustrated. Finger pointing begins.

Often, in young companies, a hero will step in, document all the objectives and tasks of the project, and then drive it to completion. Most experienced leaders recognize this can last only so long as the hero avoids burnout. If the fundamentals of developing and managing a project are not instilled organization-wide, the project will eventually fade away.

Let's start with a key question that Mark Morgan poses in his best-selling book *Executing Your Strategy*: "How important is the lowly project?"

> What a company is doing—its de facto strategy—can be summed up by identifying the group of projects in which it invests. In fact, for the espoused strategy to become a reality, it must first be converted into the packets of work we call *projects*. Projects are the temporary initiatives that companies put into place alongside their ongoing operations in order to achieve specific goals. They are clearly defined packages of work, bound by deadlines and endowed with resources, including budgets, people, and facilities.

The project—the lowly project—is the true traction point for strategic execution. It is the project that builds new products, new services, new systems, new skills, new alliances, or new delivery mechanisms for internal or external customers.[1]

The project translates high level ideas and goals into actionable, understandable work in the form of tasks or commitments that we'll expand on in the doing.

Intellectually everyone knows this, but in practice leaders often fail to make certain projects are developed, documented, and tracked.

The project, as it turns out, brings to life all the hours of planning up to this point. Yes, there is still action to take once a project is fleshed out, but the project documentation framework is critical to taking action. As noted earlier, we say the project development process is "the rubber meeting the road," because, at least with some groups, it imparts a *can we really do this* reality to the planning by addressing the typically scarce resources of people, time, money, and equipment, bringing these considerations to the foreground.

By engaging in project discussion, leaders and their people make difficult choices regarding where they will commit the resources of people, energy, time, and money, and most important, where they will not. With this in mind, let's turn to the steps of mapping a project using the template located on page 40.

Bill, our financial adviser, developed the following project. Using the MBD template discussed in chapter 3, Bill had listed the group's number one MBD on the MBD line. Notice under the heading *Goal: Deliverable*, he got *real* with his idea by writing it in the what-by-when format. Bill did this when he decided he would increase assets under management by $20 million by the end of the year. Now he had a what-by-when goal/deliverable and was ready for the next step: finding one or more pathways that were ways to achieve his goal. You'll notice he came up with the following three ways he might reach the goal:

Pathways

1. increase assets managed from each client,

2. get referrals from existing clients, and

3. seek new blood.

After he listed these three pathways, Bill and his group began to see the pathway discussion as a great way to discuss whether they had the resources, energy, and time to accomplish each goal. He later commented that he was surprised at how much there was to do in the goal-setting step and added, "I began to realize how unsupportive our environment had been to all of our employees, including myself. Heroes had made things work, but they could no longer sustain the energy level to work through our self-imposed obstacles."

Now that he had his pathways, he was ready to develop a project. You may have observed that each pathway could become a separate project. A project, which is a package of work that allows us to achieve a given goal, is defined as a set of deliverables that will be accomplished by a defined set of tasks or commitments to which resources and time have been allocated.

Pathway Projects

Project: _____ Owner: _____

Deliverable: _____ Inception Date: _____
_____ Deliverable Date: _____

Resources: _____

_____

Tasks:	Owner	Due Date
1.		
2.		
3.		
4.		
5.		
6.		
7.		
8.		
9.		
10.		

Here is an example of a completed MBD to project template:

Pathway Projects		

Project: **SEEK NEW BLOOD**		Owner: **BILL**
Deliverable: **Have 20 new client relationships by year end.**	Inception Date: **Jan 3**	
	Deliverable Date: **Dec 28**	

Resources: **Marissa / Kevin**

millennial prospect list

Tasks:	Owner	Due Date
1. Narrow down target list	Bill	1/20
2. Develop marketing campaign and scripts	Bill	1/31
3. Obtain manager approval	Bill	2/5
4. Assign call lists to resources	Bill	2/10
5. Set call schedule	Marissa	2/15
6. Begin campaign	ALL	2/16
7. Monitor and track results	Kevin	ongoing
8.		
9.		
10.		

Resources: By whom will this be done? What other resources might be needed? Notice he listed these above to the right of each task.

In this case, Bill was the owner and driver of the project. Resources for this project were discussed in a meeting and then listed. Tasks were noted in what-by-when format for the project. In follow-up meetings, Bill would both report his progress and ask Susan, Mark, and Gary to report the status of their piece of the project as green, yellow, or red. Green would denote the person was on time, with no breakdowns noted at that point. Yellow would indicate he or she was behind on one or more deliverables. Red indicated he or she was stuck at some point and needed support. Bill asked that people simply report the truth as to the status of their projects, so that he would not be surprised down the road and so that he could support them.

Alan Mulally, former CEO of Ford, met weekly with his executives to track and manage their projects using the green, yellow, and red system. He became well known for rewarding honesty about the status of projects and for punishing those who tried to hide problems. It took a while, but soon executives were openly sharing where they were having problems and subsequently receiving suggestions and support to get back on track with a project.

While Mulally was leading Ford to profit and stability, leadership at General Motors was suppressing information about various project breakdowns, among other things, and thus failing to deal with serious problems that caused driver injuries. As a result, the company ultimately faced recalls and lawsuits from their customers.

When it comes to projects, key factors to the success of individual leaders, teams, and the organization are, in large part, the following:

1. How well projects are documented, including clear ownership with deliverable dates

2. How well the people who manage the various projects determine which projects will be done and which will not be done

3. Whether project leaders and their team members openly share the status of their project, rather than trying to hide breakdowns

4. How well the project leader and team members support others in the delivery process

Summary

We began the chapter exploring the importance of the project, defined as packets of work, deadlines and allotted resources, including budgets, people, and facilities designed to help us reach our goal. The critical importance of the element project cannot be overemphasized, as it translates high-level ideas and goals into actionable, understandable work in the form of tasks.

CHAPTER 6

From Project to Doing

Congratulations! It is time to begin doing, or executing, your projects.

You have worked your way down the road map and have documented your projects. Or perhaps you had a project ready to go and jumped in here at the section on doing.

In this chapter we examine where strategy execution, in the form of delivering on projects, fails or succeeds. We explore what is often missing and needed—but is invisible—when it comes to turning projects into action and results. Up to this point, we have been action planning and living in ideas land. Now it is time to begin getting things done. This is where the rubber meets the road, so to speak. When the rubber is not on the road, the car won't move forward in the direction intended by the driver.

Some leaders are great with ideas and planning but fail to execute, experiencing some of the productivity breakdowns listed below:

1. Confusion regarding goals
2. Communication breakdowns and upsets
3. Inability to get people to do "their job"
4. Failure to deliver on promises
5. Excessive energy and time spent resolving issues
6. Lack of camaraderie: political infighting / personality clashes
7. Poor cooperation and coordination
8. Excessive personal conversations, e-mailing, or texting
9. Tardiness to meetings
10. Lowered energy, poor morale, and burnout

I know that you are bright, energetic, ambitious, and way too busy. You're paid to get things done. Some things you can do yourself, while others need the efforts of others. Consider that the higher you go in management or the larger your business becomes, the more you will be dependent on others, relying on them for key deliverables. The problems listed above come into play in a variety of ways when we are dependent on others, thereby slowing or stopping productivity. The antidote is having a bulletproof productivity system that will serve you in dealing with these issues or adroitly avoiding them throughout the rest of your career.

Assignments and projects typically come to you; you get energized and go to work. Then you have problems getting people to deliver and be accountable. You may know why you're having problems; then again, you may not have a clue.

If we were betting men, we'd wager that you do not have a complete productivity system that will support you as you go from high-level goals to great results. Very few people do, at least one they can articulate, but do not take this comment as criticism. Those of us who start our own company just jump in, doing things that have to be done. Some of us haven't been trained to lead but find ourselves in leadership positions. Larger corporations, that used to provide very effective training, have cut back on their leadership and management training programs. Bottom line, for whatever reason, you simply have not been provided (or sought out) leadership training that would serve you navigating in today's complex environment.

John was an outstanding technical lead who consistently got projects finished and out the door. Then he was promoted to manager, and his earlier success reinforced his notion that he could manage at his new level. Unfortunately, he didn't have the right skill set for his new role with its attendant jumps in scope and responsibility and after several months was in the process of crashing when we began to coach him. Each promotion with its change in scope was based on his previous success. However, no one had ever addressed the issue of new skills and competencies he might need to succeed at new levels. After assessing his skills, we informed John that, despite the fact that he had some effective skills, if he continued to do what he'd always done, he'd fail.

John got it, and we began the coaching by telling a story. As children, we used to play with a game called Mr. Potato Head. The object was to make the funniest face and body out of a potato. A variety of legs, arms, ears, eyes, and noses were provided that players could mix and match in comic combinations. We would be rolling on the floor laughing at some of the faces we created.

Now that you are intent on getting something done, John, you probably don't have time to play with potatoes. But whether you realize it or not, you probably still play mix and match as you manage day to day. You see, the process of leading and managing has multiple components to it that must seamlessly work together to get excellent results.

Components are typically linked to your managerial system. However, if any of the components are either missing, out of order, or simply wrong, you will not get optimal results—and you will not know why. This can be disastrous for your productivity, your career, and your personal well-being. The good news is that we will share and discuss some of the key components of a solid managerial system designed to help you produce effectively every time. John smiled as he realized he needed to learn some things that he didn't *know* he didn't know.

As with John, the opportunity here is to become aware of your leadership and management system, or lack of same, and to assess whether it is serving you in today's work world. Then, if you desire and see the need, you can *consciously design* your productivity system using the proven perspective, positioning notions, and conversation tools that we will present here and in the following pages. Our intention is to have you increase your productivity in whatever business situation you find yourself. Those of you who manage in various-sized businesses will up your perceived value, elevate your promotability, and increase your earning potential. Your increased worth—stemming from your ability to effectively deal with producing in a rapidly changing world that continually demands more of you while providing less—will be noticed.

In these next chapters, we're going to show you how to get what you need in order to deliver on your objectives and increase your value to your company, whatever your role. You will learn how to put all the pieces together for masterful leading. You will have an overview of our high-performance accountability system. After you work with the system a bit, you will be able to share the system with your people and get them aboard the accountability train.

In our work with hundreds of leaders over the years, we've learned that the following two things are absolutely mandatory in any endeavor, and especially when leading others:

1. You must have a proven, time-tested system for leading and managing.
2. You must work the system—that is, implement it, practice it, and reinforce others who jump in with you. This calls for consistency and persistence.

The quote below by Andre Young, CFO of Advanced Navigation and Positioning Corporation, got us all thinking at a meeting one day.

"What would it be worth to you if everyone on your team did the most important things they could do to move the goal forward each and every day?"[1]

This idea is the central focus of the doing process we're about to explore.

The section on doing is designed to help leaders in the role of producer and managers charged with production on a day-to-day basis. It's focused on executing strategy, achieving intended goals, and getting things done. We'll explore a new way of thinking and leading designed to increase productivity while growing your people and taking care of them in the process. Doing is about having a coherent production system that informs you when you need to shift or change your strategy. It is about becoming masterful in producing and innovating wherever you work.

Background

Before we go into the system, we'd like to share a follow-up letter written by Robert and our associate Randy Englund to participants of our leadership workshop. The letter includes key information on the various management models you must know about in order to be effective.

Dear Leaders,

Bottom line, our day was spent exploring and discussing your leadership and management model, which sources the explicit choices you make around

>how you set direction,
>
>how you make decisions,
>
>how you motivate, and
>
>how you coordinate activities.

We made the claim that management science has not kept up with the explosion of technology and today's global world. And we said that management as a discipline has been neglected. For the past fifty years, leadership has been glorified by gurus who have minimized the importance of management. Very simply, they have equated leadership with effectiveness and management with efficiency. Literally, the top thinks, and the rest carry out that thinking. It turns out, however, that everyone—both managers and contributors—participates in leadership and management interactions (conversations). This calls for collaboration and loosening of hierarchical constrictions. It could be said that the former is more of a centralized system, whereas the latter is more of a relational leadership system.

We're finding in our research that the exploration of management models is gaining steam. We've found that people who manage don't typically talk about or explore their management model, since it lives in the background. Day to day, they simply operate from it. Those who take a moment to examine their management model can determine the following:

1. Whether or not it is working to their advantage in their present environment and within current work demands.

2. Whether they are operating from their model because they have always done it "this way" or because "this is how we did it at my other company." We call this a *drift* and claim it is time to *design* instead.

3. Whether it would be advantageous to upgrade their management model for the sake of helping their company and themselves gain a competitive advantage.

Our focus on helping you build a successful owner's and/or managerial foundation grew out of our realization that simply sharing tips and techniques for high-performance leading and managing would be insufficient, given the challenges leaders and managers face in today's world. As noted earlier, leaders are wondering how they can keep up with competition, get visibility into all their projects, initiatives, and processes, and more rapidly determine when their strategy is not working—to mention a few concerns. Dealing with a changing workforce that manifests misplaced self-interest and failure to follow through adds to the difficulty leaders face.

An examination is required of your management frame of reference, literally the foundation of your beliefs and thinking. In *Quiet Leadership*, David Rock writes, "Improving the performance of your employees involves one of the hardest challenges in the known universe: changing the way they think."[2]

Our sense is that change starts with us, so we start by examining your paradigm or present frame of reference, reflecting on the way you think and take action.

Three Models of Leadership: Power, Process, Commitment

Donald Sull from the London School of Business has examined management models and described three basic approaches. Sull suggests that when leaders think about getting things done, three general categories come to mind.

The theme of the first is hierarchical *power* with information flowing up and commands flowing down. The main form of interaction is doing what you're told, or there are consequences.

The second approach where there are standardized operating procedures for getting things done is known as *management by process.* While this has been highly successful in reducing waste and variation, standardization tends to block innovation.

The third approach is known as managing by commitment. The view of an organization is not power or process but business as a network of promises made between people. The advantage of this approach is that it lends itself to moment-to-moment, on-the-fly situations and conversations that cannot be standardized: discussion of new strategies, addressing breakdowns, and dealing with creative opportunities.[3]

The managerial system we shared with you in the workshop, the third approach noted above, is based on using commitments to manage processes, projects, and work across units and geographies. We have found that the standard workflows and information flows that cut horizontally across organizations are missing something. That something is *people.* And when a process goes awry, we are left with very few, if any, moves to fix it.

Using the human-to-human perspective to map commitments reveals steps to locate and diagnose breakdowns (e.g., missing requests, missing commitments, missing what-by-when's, or the absence of designated accountability) and then how to intervene to fix them. The ability to map and analyze the value created or destroyed within projects, processes, initiatives, and employee networks is part of the new management model.

Absent a sense of the leader's present model—along with not knowing what other models and new ways of thinking are available—managers basically have no choice in how they proceed. With awareness, a manager can make choices about how their current model is working and choose to do something different.

We appreciate the opportunity to have worked with you and thank you for your active participation in our day together.

Best,

Robert and Randy

Summary

In this chapter we've begun to examine where strategy execution—turning your projects into results—fails or succeeds. We've explored what is often missing and needed, but invisible, when it comes to turning projects into action and results. Our intention to help you build a successful leadership foundation begins with an examination of your present management frame of reference. With this in mind, we next explored and contrasted three models of leadership, noting that we will be focusing on and encouraging use of the third—the commitment model—in chapters to come.

In the next chapters we'll go over the human-to-human commitment-based strategy implementation system, including perspective and the tools listed below:

Perspective: The Three Cornerstones—a context for your work

Tool 1: The Conversation Engine—effective coordination

Tool 2: Operating Agreements

Tool 3: Role, Responsibilities, and Authority

Tool 4: Tracking and Influencing

Tool 5: Sponsorship and Support

Tool 6: Identity, Care, and Trust

We'll begin with the three cornerstones of productivity as a simple context for your work as an owner/leader.

CHAPTER 7

The Critical Context:
The Three Cornerstones

In this chapter we'll explore a context leaders have found especially helpful for all of their productivity work.

As consultants working in the doing phase, we were routinely presented with problems and breakdowns in delivering a product or service. When we were less experienced, we had difficulty determining what was causing a given problem. Those involved were typically emotional, tending to point fingers at each other as to who was cause in the matter. We'd listen to everyone but at times became as confused as they were, thus distinctly less efficient in determining and applying an effective intervention. But over time, we began to see there were three basic areas to explore each and every time. Our premise is that the interplay of alignment, integration, and accountability pictured on the next page is central to high-performance productivity. Determining which cornerstone to explore led us quickly to the cause of a given problem or issue and to a rapid, effective intervention with satisfying results. Leaders often asked Robert, "How did you get to that intervention so quickly?" Here's what I shared with them.

Three Cornerstones

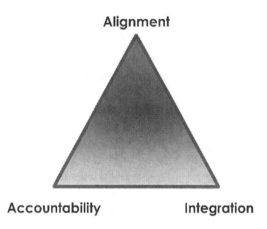

Alignment

Accountability **Integration**

Let's briefly go over each of the cornerstones so you can begin to see the invisible elements the way author Robert did.

Leaders are continually faced with interactions dealing with one or more of these cornerstones. You may be strategizing and find you need to realign on a new direction (alignment), or you may be attempting to determine whether resources are available for some new project or initiative (integration), or you may find that you are not getting something you needed that was promised (accountability).

These situations come at you point-blank, all day long. As observers, we have seen where executives are effective and where they are ineffective, causing needless waste and even adding to the problem. Leaders we observed had developed patterned ways of thinking about and discussing issues that were largely unconscious. We learned how to help these leaders in our consultations become more effective by revealing their patterned ways of thinking and talking about issues. Then we helped them develop *conversations* for dealing with breakdowns by continuously aligning and realigning on goals, supporting each other as internal customers handling each other's dependencies, and dealing with the *too-much-to-do* phenomenon and delivering as promised.

Now let's take a look at each of the cornerstones, so that you will have the same context we bring to each engagement.

The Alignment Cornerstone

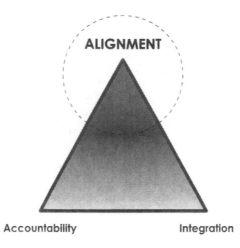

We all know that we need to be aligned and that we shouldn't even have to talk about it, but both authors run into alignment issues daily. The problem is that people are often working at cross-purposes, becoming misaligned, without anyone noticing until there is a major breakdown. Consider your automobile tires and wheel alignment.

We all need new tires on our cars at some point. After you have your four tires aligned, you drive out of the shop and, pun intended, the rubber literally meets the road. Your tires encounter ruts, bumps, and rocks, immediately going out of alignment. Unfortunately, you don't know that for many, many miles. Then you start to hear a bumping sound, and your dealer tells you that you have uneven wear or *cupping*. You have wasted hundreds of miles of tire wear, but you didn't know that was happening. You just assumed your wheels were aligned.

The first thing author Robert does with any strategy or productivity problem is check alignment. Beginning with the basics, he asks people to tell him the overall strategy or direction they are going, their current objectives, and the priority they have for each one. He then checks with their bosses to see if the answers match. When Robert consults up and down the organization in this way, numerous misalignment issues jump out at him, as you will see in the following situations:

1. Jerry, a high-level VP, was found to be working on the lowest priority goal. He did not seem to know that the CEO had another goal marked as the highest priority. The boss was shocked to learn about this alignment issue, having assumed that after his recent executive staff meeting, everyone was in agreement about goals and priorities.

2. We overheard the following from one of the executives who had just joined a task team comprised of members of different functions. "No one is clear as to what is expected or wanted of this team. No one has authority,

so conversations go in circles and no one knows exactly what is expected of them." This kind of waste-generating situation gets reported quite frequently. One direct report came to her boss complaining, "People around me are working at cross-purposes, going in different directions. I'm having difficulty prioritizing tasks on two projects, and I'm not sure what to work on next. Help!"

A Key Point Regarding Alignment

As noted above, leaders often assume their people are aligned. After all, in our last meeting didn't everyone agree to work on project A first and then work on project B? We spent several hours getting clear about that, so certainly we all must be going in the same direction, having the same understanding. Really? Anyone with some management experience knows this assumption can get us into big trouble. It is better to assume *we are not aligned* no matter what your people say or you perceive. You know that one of the most important things you can do is continuously assure that *everyone* is going in the same direction, but that takes time, and other priorities interfere with your checking continuously. What is needed to help you keep things on track is a simple process, which I will show you.

Actually you are even better off if you think of alignment as *aligning*, a truer representation of the actual dynamic.

Let's now turn to the second cornerstone.

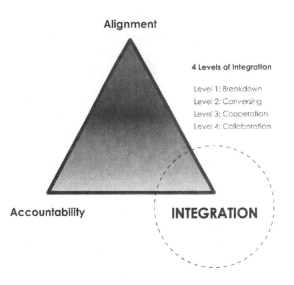

The Integration Cornerstone

The theme for integration is *cooperation*, an intention to support others with their objectives and commitments. Integration is about getting what you need and providing what others need to get things done.

Example:

> One of your executives has a manager who will not, in a timely manner, return his calls for support on

an issue critical to production. We say this is a clear lack of cooperation.

You can't get what you need from Jim, a key vendor. Your requests are ignored and your e-mails go unanswered for weeks. We say this is an integration issue, a failure to cooperate. If Jim had previously committed to return calls by a certain time, we would say we have an accountability issue.

Let's take a closer look at what we are calling integration by examining the four levels of integration.

Small groups, teams, departments, and entire companies manifest habitual ways of interacting as they go about their daily work. Integration in this sense is the way dependencies are handled. We have identified four levels of integration that range from nonproductive to highly productive.

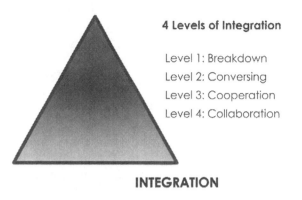

4 Levels of Integration

Level 1: Breakdown
Level 2: Conversing
Level 3: Cooperation
Level 4: Collaboration

INTEGRATION

The Four Levels

Level 1: Breakdown

The lowest level is *breakdown*. This could be characterized as a group having limited productive integration. In this type of organization, people are not getting the job done. Typical behaviors that you might see range from people hiding behind closed doors to individuals showing open hostility. If people are shouting and throwing things at each other, it's relatively easy to assess that there is a breakdown. The more subtle types of breakdown are harder to detect. Different factions meet as infrequently as possible, because "there's no point in talking to those idiots, anyway."

In one software development company, marketing and development were interacting at the breakdown level. Requests from development were met with stony silence or a yes that

79

ultimately meant no. When development people checked on the progress of a specific commitment, marketing people either did not return their call or indicated in some subtle way that they were not to be bothered.

Another company complained that a key vendor routinely failed to deliver on its promises to supply its products on time, slowing the development of the parent company's products. Work groups had tried a number of times to clear up the situation, even escalating the problem to the highest levels in the company, all to no avail. Since people needed the product, they simply tolerated the situation. This is a clear case of integration breakdown.

Typically, at this level the following complaints are heard:

1. "We don't know who should be doing what."
2. "I can't find the person I need to help me with this process."
3. "That group simply ignores our requests."
4. "We simply do not talk to them anymore."

Level 2: Conversing

The next two levels are the most common. The *conversing* level achieves basic dialogue between parties. However, there are usually hidden agendas. Although people are having conversations, there is little agreement, follow-through, or production. Often people tell us they are frustrated and feel thwarted in their attempts to coordinate action to produce their deliverables. This level is characterized by lots of talking with little result. People at this level complain that they don't get out as much as they put in.

Turf wars are a likely occurrence at this level. For example, a meeting takes place between the marketing and engineering departments. The marketing department explains what they perceive as the customer's needs. Engineering counters with their ideas, which may or may not be similar to those presented by marketing. In the end, there is little agreement.

Comments about integration at this level include the following:

1. "Every time we think we've come to an understanding with Group A, the same issue comes up again."
2. "They continually surprise us by not delivering and always have excuses."
3. "We talked with that group, but we clearly have different agendas."
4. "We blame each other, pointing fingers and don't fix things."
5. "We can't get what we want from manufacturing which leads to one of us having to do the work."

Level 3: Cooperation

Cooperation is the third level on the scale. It is the place where most organizations will be happy. There is reasonable productivity, and the environment is generally a pleasant one in which to work. Groups that work together understand the requirements of their fellow departments and agree to work within those constraints. The Engineering department *tells* the Quality Assurance department what they will produce and what will need testing. The QA department *tells* the Engineering department what their standards are and how much time it will take. Departments agree on their respective requirements and cooperate to achieve their goals.

Assessments about this level include the following:

1. "I am able to go to the person I need to get help with my project. This saves me time and wasted energy trying to figure it out myself."
2. "When groups or individuals are unable to deliver as they promised, they let me know ahead of time."
3. "When there is a breakdown, we focus on the solution rather than pointing fingers."

4. "We could improve our competence in thinking together and our willingness to be influenced by other groups and departments. We still tend to fight for our own ideas."

5. "While we're fairly clear about our requests, we could improve in this area. Also, we could improve in our ability to negotiate requests, so that we don't overburden our people. It's often easier to simply say yes, but we may have too much to do."

Level 4: Collaboration

The highest level is *collaboration*. At this level groups work together to formulate a collective approach to production, innovation, and problem solving. Collaboration is characterized more by *asking* than *telling*. Conversations could be called *dialogues* as groups seek to understand each other's ideas and needs. There is no fear or hesitation in revealing what your group needs, thinks, or is capable of accomplishing. Each group is free to offer ideas that go beyond their own area. Through greater mutual knowledge, open exchange, and integration, solutions are created that would not be possible if each group were limited only to the knowledge and resources in its own area.

In our work, we find the groups and teams that work at the collaborative level typically say the following:

1. "We can speak openly; people listen and then tell us their ideas. There is an open exchange and a healthy interaction."

2. "People think about what was said. Even though we argue at times, we are able to influence each other's thinking."

3. "I can count on people in this group to let me know if they have a problem with some deliverable or are going to be late. Also, people let me know if something has changed regarding a deliverable they have requested of me. This lets me change my priority for the deliverable, and it is very considerate of the person who made the request."

4. "This is a satisfying place to work. I enjoy working here, because I feel a part of the process rather than just taking orders."

Where You Are Now: The Integration Assessment

Typically, the *integration assessment* is administered to work units, cross-functional teams, or entire departments. Individuals are asked to answer questions focused on group-to-group integration where they have dependencies for producing products or services.

The survey reveals the general level of integration between various units and highlights pockets of higher and lower functioning. Additionally, the survey reveals specific areas the group can address to improve integration and move to the next level of conversational functionality. The survey is also a teaching tool through which people begin to see what it takes to have a highly collaborative, smoothly functioning work experience.

Recently, members of a Quality Assessment group assessed themselves following a software release. Results indicated they were usually integrating at level 3 (cooperation); however, integration with several groups was at level 2 (conversing) and even down to level 1 (breakdown).

For interactions at the lower levels, they reported they could not get what they needed in a timely manner from several groups and thus had to produce their own version of something another group was responsible for delivering. They were frustrated and exhausted, having to spend extra precious resources and energy in the process of meeting their deadlines. While they did in fact meet their deadlines, by project's end they were exhausted.

When the consultant provided the group with the results of their survey, they acknowledged the problems with certain groups and expressed strong feelings about how difficult it was to produce, given their dependencies with certain groups, Even so, they were resigned to the notion that nothing would change.

After discussing the situation at length, the QA group declared they would work together to achieve level 4 (collaboration). This meant they could no longer tolerate breakdowns at lower levels, but rather they would address issues, processes, and procedures. With the help of the consultant and the backing of their boss, they agreed to have an integration team meet to determine next steps and to institute the Committed Communication system (covered in chapter 9) to increase accountability over the next nine months.

The entire group left the meeting highly energized, having some sense that they could change things over time while moving to a new level of integration.

When management and individual contributors jointly declare their intention to develop their integration competencies and achieve level 4, the unit is on its way. While level 3 is the place where there is reasonable productivity, and the environment is generally a pleasant one in which to work, we have found that this level is not a high enough goal to strive for. Cooperation (level 3) is certainly valued and things get done, but the next level, collaboration, is evidenced by people sharing ideas or thinking together, which leads to innovation along with productivity.

The *Integration Assessment,* which my group used to check critical dependencies and the status of important relationships, served well to facilitate identifying weak areas that required action plans for improving communication and team integration performance. This tool was of great value. Applying the tool enables teams to become more aware of how interdependent they are and the impact they have on each other's contribution to results. It certainly helps build a sense of "one team" and contributes to improved operations and effectiveness.[1]

Now let's take a look at our third cornerstone, accountability.

The Accountability Cornerstone

The theme for accountability is commitment, people making and keeping commitments to meet with you, to deliver some product, to contact someone, and so on. This of course must be modeled by leaders by making and keeping commitments to their people and others.

In the accountability culture, what is promised is delivered, or the internal customer is informed about some delay. Individuals rarely complete complex projects alone. Rather, they are dependent on others and must coordinate their own and others' efforts. In some companies, we have observed that people routinely fail to keep their commitments, leading to frustration and breakdowns.

Examples of breakdowns:

1. Your executive, Larry, promised to give you his report by Wednesday, and now it is Thursday noon and there is no report. You have to call or e-mail him, which is a form of waste and a cause of some annoyance. You may even lose energy in the process.

2. Mary, another person on your staff, said she would set up a meeting with you and two other people by Tuesday. This hasn't happened, and you haven't heard from her.

We will be going deeper into the accountability cornerstone in some detail in the next chapter when we discuss the Conversation Engine.

We noted above that productivity could be thought of as a function of the interplay of alignment, integration, and accountability and that if one element is out of sync, the others are too. For example, people can be aligned but unable to get others' cooperation and thus can't deliver on their promises. People seem to be supportive and make a commitment, but then they don't deliver (accountability cornerstone). Or people can be supportive and committed and misdirected (alignment).

One manager, after learning about the three cornerstones, was in a meeting with six other managers and sensed tension was building. He suddenly realized they were arguing over some point, but they were not clear on the goal of the project. He mentally checked the cornerstones and then said, "Hey, guys, we're all arguing, and I just realized I'm not aligned with some of you as to what we really have to get done here." They all stopped arguing and moved to get clear on the project goal. The meeting went smoothly from that point.

Consider that everything you work on with others day in and day out lies within these three cornerstones. You will see as we progress that the cornerstones will be your first checkpoint when something is not going as you planned. You can quickly pinpoint the cornerstone that is out and have a conversation to make some correction. Our intention is to establish a baseline for various work groups and departments regarding which of the four levels they are working in at present. Interventions are designed to reduce roadblocks to working together while shifting to the next level of productivity. As work units move to higher levels of integration, cycle time is reduced, quality improves, and, most critically, employee energy, satisfaction, and morale are greatly enhanced.

Summary

We ask you to consider that the interplay of alignment, integration, and accountability is central to high-performance productivity. We've introduced the three cornerstones of productivity as the context for your work as a leader. Context is defined as the circumstances that form the setting for an event, statement, or idea that can be fully understood and assessed. Context literally provides meaning: how things appear to us, what we say, and what actions we take. For example, using the cornerstones as our context in consulting gave us a quick insight into the cause of a given problem or issue and led to a rapid, effective intervention and satisfying results. In our next chapters, you will see how the cornerstones can guide you in your work as we move into the doing, especially when things go awry.

CHAPTER 8

Your Ideal Week:
Shifting from Drifting to Designing

You have worked your way into the future circle shown below, and you have now documented at least one project on your project template. It is time for doing, executing your project by moving into circle 3. In this and the next chapters we are addressing the points at which the execution of strategy, in the form of delivering on projects, fails or succeeds. We're exploring what is often missing and needed—but invisible—when it comes to turning projects into action and results.

Our purpose in this chapter is to introduce a structure for doing that will fully support you in getting done the things you know need to get done.

Doing is an interesting phenomenon that includes time, action, and accountability. There is some action that needs to take place, and there is a time, or period of time, in which that action must be taken. Also, people need to do what they say they will do in that period of time. In this context, we will also discuss the notions of *design* and *drift*.

Regarding time, we know it keeps ticking away and that we can either plan our time or have no plan for using our time—but either way, it moves on. When we plan and then follow that plan, we say we are working by design. Having no plan or not following a plan results in what we call drift.

Also, when we look at time, we know there are three common distinctions, which are as follows:

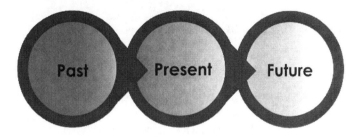

The present, which we designate as now, is either a moment in time, like right now, or a period of time we allocate for some activity. So our first point is that the ideal week will have a *right now*, which is a period of time we document on our ideal-week template for accomplishing something. For example, you might block in the time period 2:00 p.m. to 4:00 p.m. Monday for reviewing ideas to expand your business. The result of this right now is use the time to determine three options to present to your team for discussion. Often we talk about something like starting or expanding our business. When we fail to have a right now on our ideal-week worksheet, we're living in ideas land, and our new business or expansion goal will languish. Having a right now scheduled is the first step in accountability, because we have actually implied or overtly promised to another entity that we will do what we planned. Lacking a right now reveals immediately that there is no strong intention to get into action with a clear goal in mind.

This is so important that we're going to repeat it. Writing a right-now period of time on your ideal-week worksheet to indicate that you have said you would do something at the time indicated is the first step toward working in an accountability system. The other alternative is to drift into doing whatever you choose at the moment for however long you feel like doing it.

You can hold the right-now periods of time on your ideal week as commitments to actually do what you said you would do. Like many of our clients, all the authors have, at times, resisted doing what we preach. You may find that you and others will resist this process, possibly because you are moving ever closer to action—actually doing something. In our next chapter, we will be delving in more depth into being accountable and keeping your word, but for now we just want to alert you to the possibility of holding your right-now periods of time as commitments to do something.

Another key point we need to recognize is that you always have other things to do, so you need to be aware that there are things you are doing in the moment and there are things you are not doing in the moment. You have declared that you are not doing any of the other things you may have thought of while working on your right-now item. Your focus now is exclusively on the one action you have scheduled for this specific period of time. You can design your series of right-now time periods by documenting a day and time period you will address to a given issue or project and not doing anything else. Mark, one of our clients, said, "The idea of dedicating myself fully to a task at a given time sounds more like a commitment than anything to do with time." In a sense, he's right; it is a form of commitment to do what you said you would do, when you said you would do it. However, writing it on your ideal-week template is the first step in designing your week to assure you designate time to do the new project, as opposed to just drifting along doing whatever you do, letting the new project languish.

Right now author Reinhardt is correcting chapters of this book following a first editing. He had dedicated a right now by writing into his ideal-week template to clean up at least four chapters on Thursday from 1:00 p.m. to 4:00 p.m. And he is not doing anything else. He declared that he was not checking e-mail, cell phone, or responding to someone's request. Somehow he is feeling free and focused in the moment to be present just to this writing and to you, the reader.

When we don't dedicate a time period to do something, we often get going on several things at once, running around the office and accomplishing little. Plus, we get frustrated at times. When you are doing your right-now item, great ideas and other possible projects will pop into your mind, attempting to seduce you into changing your focus. That is when you need to remind yourself exactly what *this specific* right now is dedicated to accomplishing and for whom it will serve.

An Exercise:

Let's assume you want to design your week so that you use your time more efficiently and effectively. Where do you start?

First you need to determine what you want on your ideal-week worksheet.

You can start by looking at how you are using your time at the present. Start with a weekly calendar printed out or on your computer, and begin analyzing how many hours you are at work. You might break down your work time for the current week into training, marketing, planning, servicing, preparation, presentation, researching, workshops, and committee meetings—all part of the basic functions of your job. You can also check on how much time you are spending in community activities. How much time do you spend exercising? How about family time, including weekends? Mark down the hours spent on each activity, and map it all on a blank weekly sheet.

Now go back four weeks, and repeat the process for each of those weeks. See what shows up about your patterns. Where is your consistency? Now you can see how satisfied you are with your week overall, and you can locate areas you would like to address.

Here is a sample of various activities you can check:

1. Training or teaching

2. Planning

3. Marketing

4. Researching

5. Giving presentations

6. Working up plans or projects

7. Meeting with clients or providing service

8. Conducting workshops or committee meetings

9. Reviewing

10. Budgeting/financial planning

11. Designing

12. Writing/reading

13. Using e-mail/Facebook/Twitter

	Monday	Tuesday	Wednesday	Thursday	Friday	Saturday	Sunday
5:00 AM							
6:00 AM	Workout	Workout	Workout	Workout	Workout	Workout	
7:00 AM	Faith	Faith	Education	Faith	Faith		
8:00 AM	W.P.	Appointments		Appointments	W.P.	OFF TIME	Family
9:00 AM							
10:00 AM							Church
11:00 AM							
12:00 PM			Community				Family
1:00 PM	Organize						
2:00 PM							
3:00 PM			Organize		OFF TIME		
4:00 PM							OFF TIME
5:00 PM	Family	Family	Family		Family	DATE NITE	
6:00 PM				Presentations			
7:00 PM							
8:00 PM							
9:00 PM							
10:00 PM							
11:00 PM							

Exercise:

Let's take a look at what you want your future ideal week to look like. Based on the regular activities that you've checked for the last four weeks, see what you want to change. Then begin to fill in the ideal-week sheet designating time for your various activities. Be sure to get any new project on your ideal-week sheet, or you can count on it not getting started.

Below is a blank ideal-week template, and you can also download the ideal-week template from our website, www .lauridsenreinhardtgroup.com.

	Monday	Tuesday	Wednesday	Thursday	Friday	Saturday	Sunday
5:00 AM							
6:00 AM							
7:00 AM							
8:00 AM							
9:00 AM							
10:00 AM							
11:00 AM							
12:00 PM							
1:00 PM							
2:00 PM							
3:00 PM							
4:00 PM							
5:00 PM							
6:00 PM							
7:00 PM							
8:00 PM							
9:00 PM							
10:00 PM							
11:00 PM							

When you are done filling in your week, step back and take a look at your week. Could this be your ideal week? Let's test it. Keep it as a master schedule in front of you and consider being guided by it. Remember—your ideal week can always be adjusted. Let the ideal week propel you into the future with more efficient time use and a much more enjoyable life.

Author Reinhardt has said, "Controlling your own time is critical to your success; don't let time run away from you. This is where your ideal week can serve you by letting you know what you are working this week and next week. This is critical to designing your life. Life is a journey—plan your journey. Remember the words of Cervantes, the Spanish writer: 'The journey is better than the inn (destination). Enjoy the journey; look back with satisfaction.'"

Summary

In this chapter we addressed a key turning point at which the execution of strategy—in the form of delivering on projects—fails or succeeds right at the beginning of your efforts. We've found this step is often missing and needed, but invisible; thus, its absence goes unnoticed.

We offered that doing is an interesting phenomenon that includes time, action, and accountability. There is some action that needs to take place, and there is a time, or period of time, in which that action must be taken. Also, people need to do what they say they will do in that period of time. We introduced the notions of design and drift, indicating you will get far more done when you design your week.

In our part 3, armed with your ideal week and a right-now time to work on your project, we'll move on to the doing and continue with accountability.

PART 3

The Doing

CHAPTER 9

Doing with Commitment: Consistently Creating Intended Results

Now that you have a project documented and your ideal week has a block of time allotted for that project, you are ready for action. Remember—when it comes to taking action and getting results, planning is just a first step:

"If all you do is sit around and visualize and plan, the men in the overalls with the big trucks will come and take away your furniture!"[1]

Of course we don't want the furniture to be taken away, so let's talk action.

Leaders and managers typically determine or are assigned a project, and being action oriented, they roll up their sleeves and jump into doing things. We know we've done that all too many times. We're recommending you do something very different that will set you up to optimize your chances of success by positioning the activities of doing any project in a context of commitment and accountability. Our purpose in this chapter is to clarify what we mean by that and to present the difference between just doing things and doing things in a commitment context.[2]

A Note on Perspective

Business can be thought of as a game that is oriented toward the future. Part of the purpose of the game is to provide continuous customer satisfaction that opens the possibility of an ongoing working relationship. Every time we produce satisfaction, we build trust with our customer, and that trust, in turn, strengthens the relationship. Contented customers are at least partially a function of our effectiveness in fulfilling their conditions of satisfaction. In other words, did we produce what we intended and the customer desired?

Consider that we can only accomplish this when people within the business work together to fulfill promises to each other and to paying customers. Our effectiveness in working together internally is measured by these standards:

1. Responsiveness
2. Customer satisfaction

3. Profitability

4. Employee satisfaction

Each of these standards is driven by our effectiveness at ultimately fulfilling each customer's conditions of satisfaction through our support for each other during the process of delivery. And the key point we want to make is that leaders and their people need a system to guide them in both delivering and supporting each other's productivity.

You may view your business, whether solo or with a number of others, in several ways. If you have several people working together, you may view your business as various groups, teams, or even clusters of individuals working together. No matter how many people work with or for you, we'd like you to consider that any business (even a solo one) can be viewed as a network of conversations designed to fulfill the delivery of products and services to customers.

This perspective offers a view of work as interactions among skilled, experienced, creative individuals with clear accountabilities, rather than as a series of tasks connected by inputs and outputs. Day-to-day, moment-to-moment, people are sharing information, exercising judgment, committing themselves, and taking action, even as they improvise and invent new ways of doing things in the midst of unexpected circumstances that inevitably arise.

The three axioms guiding us are as follows:

1. The work of managers and contributors happens in conversation.
2. The basic or key unit of communication in work is commitment.
3. The basic structure of managerial and individual contributor work is the conversational network.

The consequence of this interpretation of work is that center stage is given to people and their concerns, including the way they think, learn, collaborate, interact with each other, and deal with changes in their environment. Conversely, in the traditional or more commonsense approach, center stage is given to things and data.

The more effectively managers and contributors manage the basic set of conversations (based in commitments) that recur in their work, the more productive their units will be. When the conversational interactions and commitments between leaders, teams, or individuals are ineffective, the result is

- inaction,

- lack of accountability,

- poor decisions,

- redundancy,

- weak or missing collaboration,

- misallocated resources, and

- mistrust.

This creates waste and lost value to the project team and, ultimately, the organization.

Based on this interpretation or perspective, we will be sharing some proven conversational tools (skills) that will fully support you, whether you are a solo enterprise or have a large number of people working together in your organization.

Our Experience with High-Performing Cultures

In our work with companies, we have come across leaders and managers who have developed what we call a high-performing culture. Products get out on time with all promised features delivered. People have clear deliverables; roles and responsibilities are defined so that all persons know what is expected of them. The decisions each individual can make and not make are understood.

There are unwritten rules for how people work together: that is, everyone knows what others will do and what they will not do in their interactions. People alert each other to breakdowns and come up with interventions or solutions. They are willing to confront various issues and differences in a direct yet supportive manner. When blocked in any way, a team member can get a power source or sponsor to help them get back into action.

The team or unit is a community, although the members may not think of themselves this way. They have coevolved to the present state and typically do not even know why they are so productive, innovative, and satisfied with the part they have played in doing the work. When we observe them, we notice they are supportive and go out of their way to help one another. Competition is neither in the foreground nor problematic in this culture. Typically these groups are collocated and have worked together for a number of years. Those individuals who didn't fit in have left, and others more open to the ways in which the group intends to work have joined. Oh, and did I mention that people love to work in these environments?

According to people we've interviewed, the preceding situations have not come about by conscious design. Rather, they happened over time with no one predicting or declaring how the group members would interact down the road. What we might call *respectful communication* just seemed to happen. Here is the key fact we learned from countless interviews: the teams and units that had worked together for more than fifteen years had unwittingly developed an unspoken commitment system. The invisible system acted as a context for all their actions, communications, expressions of emotion, and decisions. No one realized what had happened. They just knew it worked, and they liked working together.

This is all well and good, but as we've noted, conditions have changed. Now we rarely get to work with a collocated team for such a lengthy period of time. Rather than having fifteen years to evolve, we see virtual teams cobbled together across countries and assigned demanding project deadlines. We hear complaints from those who cannot get critical assignments, requirements, deliveries, and handoffs handled—and from people who cannot even get a phone call returned. We need to speed things up, consciously designing how we will interact to produce our products and services. We can't leave the development of a commitment-based culture up to chance. The idea of actively developing a commitment-based culture grew out of our work with frustrated clients who complained that they could not reliably get their work done.

As our consulting services moved us in and out of large, medium, and small companies, we noticed similar breakdowns and issues when it came to producing on goals and executing strategy. With feedback from our clients, we began to develop a system that would address today's unique leadership and managerial challenges.

First, let's take a look at that key tool we mentioned earlier, what we call the *conversation engine*, a communication process that drives the three cornerstones of productivity.

The Overlooked Crucial Performance Driver

Leaders have noted that the cornerstones of productivity have helped them quickly locate areas of breakdown, but they've also found the cornerstones are not sufficient by themselves to drive strategy and productivity conversations. A crucial performance driver has been overlooked over the years. It is an engine that will help you drive the interplay of the three cornerstones and dramatically improve the way people interact within executive teams, project teams, or groups, as well as across functions, with other companies, and even virtually (via media), whether with customers, suppliers, or partners.

The Missing Communication System

Alignment

Accountability   Integration

Our purpose in this section is to give you a high-level view of the missing system or set of tools comprising what we call committed communication. The critical element of this system of communicating is the *conversation engine,* located at the center of the triangle above. The conversation engine will help you to continuously deal with and maintain an aligned, integrated, and accountable team, business unit, or company. As noted, we began to see in our consulting work that we needed a communication or interaction system to effectively drive the interplay that allows leaders to deal with breakdowns. They can do this by continuously aligning on goals, dealing with "too much to do," making decisions, supporting colleagues as internal customers handling each other's dependencies, and delivering as promised. Bottom line, we wanted to help leaders navigate the sea of conversations that make up their day.

The Conversation Engine

Let's take a look at what has proven to be such an effective part of the basic system of interacting—the conversation engine. With your concerns and issues in mind, we'll explore this conversation engine and the perspective that acts as a driver for all conversations.

We've learned from experience that you will not master the conversation engine at the level needed to implement it in your work simply by reading about it. Therefore we recommend that you check out our recorded free webinar at www.lauridsenreinhardtgroup. com. This will provide a deeper understanding of what some people have called a powerful, effective, yet counterintuitive way to sweep people up into being accountable and taking care of each other.

With this in mind, please consider the following as simply an overview of the conversation engine.

We have observed a specific set of conversations used by people who produce consistent customer satisfaction. Learning these moves is not the same thing as learning a new technique. Instead, it requires developing a different orientation toward action and business. This new orientation allows you to see the game of business in a new light and to bring a new understanding to the phenomenon of mobilizing action and generating customer satisfaction.

The purpose of this section is to lay out a new way to see action, produce satisfaction, and become more effective at mobilizing action and taking care of your customers, no matter what their level in the company.

Whenever we produce satisfaction in any business, it is possible to observe some essential steps or *conversational moves* taking place. These universal basic moves are captured in what we call the conversation engine, based on communication techniques developed by Fernando Flores.

Let's take a look at how this system works. As a leader, when you are in charge of an initiative or project, you typically make requests of your people. We often observe that people ask for things, but then do not provide a time by which they need the deliverable. The key to requests is to remember to include a *what by when* in each request, so that the person you are asking knows clearly what you want and by when you would like it, if possible.

Your Interactions:
Producing value between people

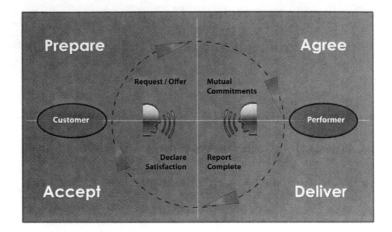

As depicted above, the person you are asking to do something for you (the performer) can respond in one of four primary ways, each of which is considered a commitment. They can take responsibility for the request by

- making a commitment to complete it (yes);

- refusing for whatever reason (decline);

- suggesting an alternative action or negotiation (make a counter-offer); or

- committing to commit by telling you they need to talk with someone or get more information and then designating a day and time when they will let you know.

Our anecdotal research into coordination of action reveals that when groups are working smoothly, productively, and harmoniously, their members are using these four primary ways of responding to each other, although often unwittingly. They have little conscious understanding of what makes up an effective, productive, and satisfying interaction; thus, they really don't know why a given interaction works so well sometimes and at other times does not.

With the conversation engine model under your wing, you will be listening for the primary responses that we call *language actions* in your verbal exchanges. Armed with this tool you will be able to understand and identity what is working, what is not, and why.

Recently, a manager named Mark met with John, his lead technical supervisor. He asked him to take certain steps for a project that involved determination of what would be offered to one of their top customers. John, who had several other projects on his plate, told Mark, "Maybe I can get to it." Mark found John's response confusing. Had he made a commitment to him or not?

Would John actually take any action? These were the kinds of situations that kept Mark up in the middle of the night worrying about various projects.

To understand what is going on here in terms of their interaction—and how Mark needs to proceed—it's necessary to take a deeper look into the conversation engine process and the nature of requests.

Underlying all the steps in the commitment-based productivity system is the notion that managers manage *commitments* rather than activities or actions. Organizing work around commitments can provide some valuable benefits and opportunities. For one, by taking your own commitments to heart and by communicating all the information people need in order to commit to and complete your requests, you model the behavior you want your employees to follow. For another, when your people experience breakdowns in making and keeping their commitments, you learn about this firsthand because your people keep you apprised. When they don't, you know that too. This kind of knowledge can help you determine when and how to use coaching techniques to help people be accountable, solve problems, and improve performance.

Common Breakdowns
Lack of clarity, alignment, accountability and feedback

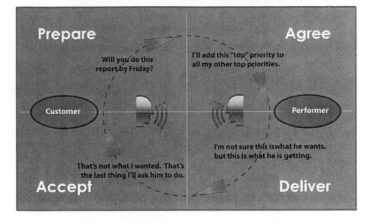

As previously noted, the conversation engine specifies four distinct phases of a conversation that, when mastered, allow managers not only to be more productive but also to quickly analyze and troubleshoot breakdowns. The ability to label the phases of their communications enables leaders to pinpoint these breakdowns. Rather than live with the mystery of what went wrong, a manager can shape responses that clarify and remedy the breakdown. This approach also trains less experienced managers to observe what is happening in their work conversations. Such training quickly improves their managerial effectiveness.

The phases of a complete cycle are as follows:

1. Request

2. Negotiate

3. Perform

4. Receive customer feedback

Units of work are accomplished by completing communication cycles. As mentioned above, we have found that we can analyze and remedy breakdowns more quickly by using the four phases as a structure for observation and a guide for troubleshooting. If a manager makes a request, for example, we might observe that the request was incomplete or misunderstood. We might determine that the person asked to do the work didn't fully understand the request. Then we could make educated guesses about the situation and take corrective action.

While the phases explained below are fairly easy to understand, we have found it takes attention and diligence to incorporate them into daily managerial observation, listening, and speaking. We have found that if you will take one phase per week and practice it, over time you will begin to naturally use them in your daily interactions

Phase 1: Request—"I'm Asking."

First, let's address phase 1, the request. People who are responsible for projects usually need support from others. This means they must make requests of coworkers or subordinates. This is phase one of a conversation based on language actions.

Some people are reluctant to make these requests, so they veil them by saying something like "It would really be nice if someone could help out on my project." Other people are more assertive and able to ask for help. Often they will delegate parts of a project. But whatever the case, we have learned in our work with managers that there is much to consider about requests and that poor or incomplete requests are a major source of waste in the form of expanded cycle time and missed deadlines.

Two areas of breakdown that we continually encounter are these:

1. Requests have no clear delivery date. In this breakdown, the person making the request leaves the date and time of delivery open, assuming that others know when they can—or should—provide the product or service.

Here is a typical example: "Joe, I'd like you to complete the proposal for Apple marketing." Joe agrees to do the work, but neither Joe nor his boss has said anything about a specific date when the proposal will be delivered. Consequently, the manager doesn't know when to start prodding Joe, if Joe doesn't deliver in a timely manner. The manager may have a required delivery date in mind, but failing to state it clearly and get Joe's agreement makes the date nonexistent for practical purposes. This kind of incomplete communication happens far too frequently, and because the people involved have different expectations, it can cause a significant amount of distress for both parties.

At times a previous conversation may have established a clear understanding about the date of delivery. Sometimes contingencies make it understood that a particular task must be completed by Friday at noon. Even so, restating the due date in each subsequent conversation is a good technique. We recommend that you always clarify a date and/or time as insurance against any misunderstanding.

Here's a note from a client VP:

> I've been paying attention to what goes on through
> the lens of the conversation engine. The big issue

here is *what by when*. My CEO is a consummate salesman. I don't know how exactly he keeps selling the clients but, for example, I talked to him today about getting my compensation package nailed down. He said, "How about Friday?" I said, "Sure." He then asked me a few other questions, and I got off the phone before I realized I didn't have a firm time on Friday!

I responded to this VP with a written note saying, "In the past you just overlooked using the what-by-when part of your requests as a standard way of operating—a habit. Now you know better because you're armed with the distinction what-by-when. By simply observing whether you get the what-by-when into the request, you will bring about a change in a long-established habit, and you will dramatically improve the rigor of your conversations. Your power, in the sense of effectiveness in getting things done, goes up."

2. The person making the request is either not sure what he or she is asking for or is not clear in making the request. We have consulted with numerous groups that have experienced this breakdown in the request process.

People making requests have conditions of satisfaction or expectations that accompany their requests. To help leaders and their teams, we make a distinction between conditions of satisfaction and the more commonly used term *deliverable*. A deliverable is typically a product or service, while a condition of satisfaction is an assessment about that product or service. McDonald's delivers a consistent, standardized hamburger—the product or deliverable. When we're in a hurry, it meets our conditions of satisfaction; when we're not rushed, we go some place that serves a more satisfying and "real" hamburger. If these distinctions are not part of the communication, however, the typical result will be misunderstanding, with all its attendant problems from confrontations to wasted effort. Often this is manifested by the statement, "This is not what I asked for."

Now let's turn to the next phase.

Phase 2: Negotiation—It's a Good Thing

We have observed many interactions between requesters and the performers of requests. In most interactions, we have noted that the requester often becomes clearer about what he or she actually wants when the performer participates by using phase two, negotiation.

In this phase, instead of automatically answering yes, the performer listens to the request and then can give one of the other three responses noted earlier, as follows:

a. "*Yes*, you can count on me to do that."

b. "*No*, you cannot count on me to do that."

c. "Let's discuss this" or *negotiate* the terms.

d. "Let me get back to you," a *commitment to commit* at a later time.

The third type of response, "Let's discuss this," signals negotiation. In this part of the interaction, the performer tries to gain clarity about what is wanted and assesses whether the request can be delivered by the date and time requested and in accordance with the conditions of satisfaction. Negotiations can turn into a yes or a no as a result of the ensuing discussion, or they can lead to the fourth response.

This kind of response, "Let me get back to you," involves setting a date for a date. The performer may have to check his or her resources and get back to the requester. In doing this, the performer sets a date and time by which he or she will get back to the requester with a yes, a no, or a further negotiation, which may involve an alternative plan of action.

We have found that certain corporate cultures do not permit a subordinate to say no. In conversations where a simple yes is appropriate, there's no problem. However, a yes is not always reasonable or even possible. What happens, then, in cultures where requests from superiors may not be refused?

We've found that in teams or units working in what we might call *command and control* cultures, the inability to give a response other than yes leads to what we call *slippage*. By this we mean people begin to choose what they will do and what they won't do or can't get to, often basing their decisions on power or political factors. In this situation, many requests are not brought to completion, even though the performer never utters the word *no*. Understanding how—and why—this dynamic works can provide an impetus for change in the corporate culture.

Even where subordinates' compliance is mandated, there may be numerous ways to manage the completion of requests. Giving employees options they can work with improves the situation for everyone—employees and bosses alike. Greater productivity and accountability can be achieved when people know how to balance commitments and to get help when they need it.

In other environments, we have seen bosses who understood the process of request and commitment well enough to look at a *no* in the context of the system. Their intent was to see what in the system prevented a highly qualified subordinate from agreeing to work on a clear, specific, and reasonable request. In this way, the elements of the conversation engine can help pinpoint system breakdowns and identify processes that may need improvement.

The negotiation phase, like any form of collaboration, involves what we call *thinking together* in partnership. During negotiation, the performer thinks through the request with the requester. In this *thinking* conversation, both parties are exploring possibilities and working together to understand each other's position and point of view.

Sometimes a modified request grows out of the process. Modifications might include pushing aside one project to free resources for a more important one. By thinking together, each person indicates his or her willingness not only to share thinking and evaluations but also *to be influenced*. For this reason, we have found that the authoritarian mode, an unwillingness to think with someone else or to be influenced by others, is deadly to realizing the full benefits of committed communication.

All right. We've made a request and dealt with the response of the performer. Now let's see how understanding this process helps Mark in his communication with Mary.

What's Going on Here?

Mark asks Mary to take action toward implementing a request he has made. Mary answers, "Maybe I can get to it." This is not a clear or satisfactory response when operating within the conversation engine model, so Mark thinks about the four responses that are part of the process (yes, no, let's negotiate, or I commit to commit later) and tries to decide which response Mary has given him. Unsure if Mary has said yes or no, Jim needs clarification. After all, this is clearly a priority project.

Using his new way of thinking, Mark determines that Mary's response (that she would try) is not a clear commitment. Remembering the first source of breakdowns—requests that have no clear delivery date—Mark asks Mary to tell him when he can expect the deliverable he has asked for. This question is designed to clear up any confusion about Mary's vague response. Three things can happen in this situation.

- The first is that Mary can simply commit to a date and time of delivery.

- The second is that Mary may have some strong consideration about being able to deliver, in which case she can bring that up with Mark and begin a negotiation. For example, she may have several other responsibilities and anticipate a lack of resources that might prevent her from delivering. If Mark so desires, he can help her sort out her priorities, offering support where needed to help her deliver. The two of them are now collaborating (thinking together) with the intention of making things work for both of them.

- The third thing that can happen typically indicates that Mary has a concern but is not sharing it with Mark. In this case, she will either continue to offer unclear responses that are variations of the "I'll try" response, or if she feels too much pressure, she might simply say yes but have no intention of fulfilling her commitment.

If someone continues to offer an "I'll try" response after you've made several attempts to pin down specifics, explore the person's concerns. Often, employees feel overloaded but are uncomfortable sharing that with you. In this case, Mark even suggests that Mary delegate the project to another manager, but Mary is unwilling to do that. If she continues to say yes to your requests and then fails to deliver without alerting you, you have a performance problem.

Phase 3: Performance: Getting to the Action

The process moves into phase 3, *performance*, once the performer commits to meeting the requester's conditions of satisfaction. In this phase, the performer, Mary, takes whatever actions are needed to complete the project or assignment.

Our cardinal rule here is: no surprises to the requester! By this we mean that if you run into problems or breakdowns in your attempts to deliver, you must alert the person who made the request and explain the delay or renegotiate the commitment you made.

Working in the conversation engine system does not mean you will always deliver on time and exactly as promised. Breakdowns happen. Things change. People you counted on leave, become ill, or fail to deliver themselves. Outside vendors can't or won't provide what you need. The main thing is to get back to your requesters. Do not surprise them. They have made commitments to others based on the commitments you made to them. In keeping commitments, you maintain positive work relationships. You sustain the hidden power and currency of your network of relationships, and you build and retain trust.

Lately, we have seen too many departments from which trust has vanished. When commitments are not honored, relationships can be damaged or broken. Product delivery dates are missed, and the viability of the company is severely threatened.

Phase 4: Don't Forget the Internal Customer!

The last but equally important phase is often omitted or overlooked in a work interaction. In this phase, the customer or requester provides feedback on the performance of the request. Based on the conditions of satisfaction, the requester makes an assessment of how well the performer delivered. The requester either acknowledges the performer for the work done or coaches the performer about corrections needed to fulfill the conditions of satisfaction to achieve a better outcome.

Summary

Our claim is that managers and contributors typically focus on the flow of information and materials along with a collection of tasks and activities. This focus on tasks and activities has led them to overlook the key dimension of human coordination that we claim shapes or influences all other elements of production processes. "In fact, when we observe people working, we find that they invent processes, work in them, change them when they need adjusting, and even replace them when they become obsolete. People do this with a structured, but implicit, set of conversations, or language actions."[3]

Some people display an *unconscious* competence with these conversations, while many others are less competent. By making these interaction processes explicit and by providing a framework for understanding the human element of coordination that underlies these interactions, we have been able to systematically reduce waste, decrease cycle time, and increase the satisfaction of both internal workers and paying customers. As previously noted, our anecdotal research into coordination of action and the conversation engine indicates that when groups are working smoothly, productively, and harmoniously, their members are using the four phases in their conversations, although often unwittingly. It's common even for people to operate within this conversational model to have little conscious understanding of what makes up an effective interaction. If problems arise, they cannot explain why a given group sometimes functions well and at other times does not.

Nevertheless, people who work in this way have an unspoken respect for one another. They realize the importance of maintaining strong, healthy work relationships. They know that in today's interdependent workplace, everyone produces within a network of conversations through which people make requests and deliver on promises. This network is where managing to produce through others begins.

By way of review, the key four responses are as follows:

1. "*Yes*, you can count on me to do that."
2. "*No*, you cannot count on me to do that."
3. "Let's discuss this" or *negotiate* the terms.
4. "Let me get back to you," a *commitment to commit* at a later time.

Finally, we can't overemphasize that the ability to use the conversation engine is one of the central factors in whether or not you actually engage your strategy.

In the next chapter, we explore a way to work with your people to encourage them to make and keep commitments.

For a more detailed description of the conversation engine process with examples, please see chapter 2 in our book *Boss Talk …* *A Manager's Guide to Exceptional Productivity and Innovation.*

CHAPTER 10

Leveraging the Power of Operating Agreements

We shared the three cornerstones of productivity, the notion of doing within a context of commitment, and a deeper discussion into the specifics of the conversation engine tool. As noted, the conversation engine is the core element in our high-performance accountability system. We found, however, that it is not enough on its own. For this reason, we'll now share an important tool you can use to position and leverage the effectiveness of the conversation engine in order to get things done consistently. You will be able to use the leverage that operating agreements provide to manage and guide your people inside a commitment context.

The Marketing and Development Breakdown

Come back with author Lauridsen in time to a cold, rainy winter day in New Jersey. His day started with a telephone call. "Can you get out here to help us immediately?" implored the director of software engineering in a Fortune 500 company. "We are at a standstill with marketing. They promise to deliver something, then ignore or forget their commitment. We need certain things from them—it's not like we're working alone on this project. We just cannot get their cooperation."

The next call came from the marketing director, who pleaded, "Please help me get development off our back. They make more requests of us than we could ever fulfill. They're never satisfied."

Pressures had mounted until, finally, one functional group was refusing to talk with the other. Obviously, the decision not to talk to another group only exacerbated the problem, because the interdependencies remained. Various needs went unfulfilled, production suffered, and morale was at an all-time low.

To address this problem, we arranged a block of time when Marketing and Software Development could meet to resolve their differences. After two hours of a fairly heated exchange of viewpoints, we asked what the members of each department wanted. We intended to find out what they were up to and what results they wanted for the company. Each person explained what he or she was doing, along with the results desired. People shared how difficult it was to get results when functional departments were battling.

After some time, the atmosphere in the room shifted dramatically as each person realized that everyone was trying to reach the same overall goal, even though individuals had different deliverables, actions, and commitments. People began to see that there was nothing wrong with them as individuals. Rather, an important yet invisible structure was missing. When there were breakdowns in communication, people had nowhere to turn. The normal elements of effective communication—cooperation, collaboration, and the coordination of action—were not in play. All people could do when they couldn't get what they needed to perform their assignments was suffer alone, be quiet, complain, or go back and ask for a deliverable once again, often facing the other group's wrath or stony silence. Not fun and not good for morale.

What Was Missing?

We call the missing element *operating agreements* or rules of the game. The two groups had never agreed upon a set of operating principles or agreements that they would adhere to that would have helped them resolve communication breakdowns. Such agreements are a mechanism for proactively determining how people will work together when collaborating and coordinating actions for the sake of accomplishing shared goals.

These agreements provide a structure or context for what people will do and not do, so that as a group or cross-functional team, they can produce effectively, handle miscommunications and other breakdowns in coordinating actions, and maintain positive work relationships at the same time. On the other hand, a failure to develop operating agreements results in a loss of the managerial leverage available to the managers to resolve issues and often leads to dramatically lowered motivation, commitment, and overall productivity. This is what had happened to the two groups.

Some leaders and managers do not understand that people perform best when they know—and help establish—the *rules of the game.* These leaders often work feverishly in a get-the-product-out-the-door or shoot-from-the-hip mentality. They do not take time to generate a set of team, group, or company-wide agreements for how their people work together or with other groups. Instead, managers handle each situation or breakdown as it comes up, often arguing to convince individuals of the necessity of doing things a certain way. In these companies, the word *chaos* doesn't come close to describing what goes on between and within groups and teams.

Why Operating Agreements Matter

Suppose you are playing soccer, and you bring in a new player who has never played the game before. Of course, this person will be hard-pressed to step smoothly into the flow of the game. The new player may have little knowledge about how to act or what to do.

We know that in game theory there is a point to the game, equipment that is allowed and not allowed, rules and guidelines for playing, and finally, a game strategy. After explaining that the point of the game is to get the ball in the other team's net and prevent that team from kicking the ball into your team's net, you still have to share the rest of the rules. If you don't, your new friend will be penalized by the referee and possibly tossed out of the game for various infractions. Each time the new player fails to follow a rule, you will have to provide additional instructions. You might call this OJT, or on-the-job training.

Developing operating agreements requires that each team member be open to participating and learning. Each member of the group must come to agree with, or at least be willing to abide by, the group's notion of how members will work together. Additionally, members of the group must be willing to make corrections in their ways of working with one another and, when guidelines are not followed, to deal with the consequences as agreed upon by the group. To learn more about working together, let's take a look at some operating guidelines.

At least in the past, most operating agreements in the military services were directives with no input from the lower ranks. With knowledge-based workers, we recommend that the group, team, or department come up with its own operating guidelines to ensure buy-in. You will find that, for the most part, people want to be productive and will come up with essentially the guidelines you would have written yourself. Once you have a set of guidelines, you and your team members simply hold each other into account. You can remind people of what everyone agreed to; then people simply have to adhere to the guidelines they agreed to follow.

As a manager, you too are part of the accountability system; thus, team members need to feel free to talk with you if you fail to live up to your commitments. This is a critical point, as there is a big difference between being bullheaded and on insisting on being right no matter what—and being open to learning from the people you manage. You will find that if you are willing to be a learner instead of a defender of your actions, your people will help you grow and develop your managerial skills.

Setting Up Operating Agreements

To set up your group's operating agreements, you'll need to have an *operating agreements* meeting with your people. Present and discuss the concept, and be sure to let them know that nothing will be decided in the first meeting and that there will be another meeting to agree to the guidelines as a group.

Have each person write down what he or she views as the most important guidelines for working together. List all these suggestions on a flip chart. Once you have everyone's input, go over the list, discussing each item to see if there is agreement. Allow for conflicting points of view by letting people talk about their concerns and insisting that all points of view are valuable and need to be considered. Remember that you can't force commitment. When people can't or won't commit, take time to discuss why they have reservations and to let them vent. People will typically realize that this process will serve them well, and they will come around.

Often the process of developing guidelines is met with resistance from certain team members. Let these people know it's okay if they don't like rules or guidelines but that, like them or not, the group needs guidelines in order to produce effectively.

As an illustration of this, consider traffic signals. What driver hasn't at one time or another been frustrated by having to wait at a red light? Yet it takes just one experience of having the electrical power knocked out by some catastrophe—whether a California earthquake, Michigan snowstorm, Florida hurricane, or Missouri flood—to demonstrate the true value of those frustrating lights. Driving home through city traffic without signals is an experience in chaos. After the Northern California earthquake in 1989, the commute home for many drivers took up to three or four times longer than usual, even though people responded graciously and safely to the conditions. Clearly, we need operating structures in society, and we need them in our work as well.

Remember that meeting between the marketing and development departments we described earlier? Guidelines were the answer there too. The marketing department and development realized how important it was to make and keep their promises to deliver. As a solution, marketing and development people agreed to do the following:

1. Treat their internal customers (each other) with the same respect and importance as external customers.

2. When development asked for something, if marketing could deliver, the department would agree upon a date and time for the delivery and work with the intention of meeting the conditions of satisfaction for the development customer. If something happened to slow down or prevent marketing from delivering, the representative would "raise their hand," alerting the development person so that adjustments could be made.

3. If the people in marketing were sure they could *not* deliver, they would help development find someone who could provide the product or service.

4. Both groups would feel free to inquire as to the status of any deliverable that had been committed to by either group. This meant that the groups were getting past the defensiveness that often comes up when we ask people how they are doing regarding their deliverables.

5. If marketing got stuck and was unable to move forward, the department would bring in a third person to help mediate. If marketing needed further help, it would call in senior management to make a decision based on priorities.

6. Everyone in marketing and development agreed that these agreements were to be in effect unless the teams agreed to change. This precluded individuals from changing their minds and operating as they preferred, rather than as the group had decided.

The marketing and development groups reported a change in attitude between the two of them almost immediately, along with a strengthened intention to serve each other rather than fight and bicker. However, we all know that behaviors do not change simply because we hold a meeting, so the consultant involved with these two groups offered a follow-up consultation to deal with any breakdowns in the system. Productivity continued to improve dramatically. The one person in marketing who refused to alter his behavior subsequently left the company.

The Operating Agreements Worksheet

We have included an operating agreements worksheet that you may copy and pass out to your people when you hold your meeting to determine how you will work together. You can also download a copy at www.lauridsenreinhardtgroup.com.

Eventually you will get buy-in for the agreements and a solid commitment from each person. If some people are unwilling to commit to the agreements, you will know who is not suited to produce effectively in your accountability culture.

The theme of operating agreements is determining "how we will get things done around here." The group will be discussing and determining such things as the following:

1. How we'll work together and treat each other
2. What we can expect from each other regarding our dependencies
3. How we will keep each other informed
4. What we can do to resolve breakdowns

The process the group uses to determine its agreements is valuable in its own right. People will be required to influence and be influenced in order to come to some agreement. When groups meet to develop agreements, the members of each group will naturally defend against the ideas and ways of others, preferring their own. It is fairly normal to have a preference for one's own thinking and ways of working. Several leaders have indicated that the interaction (give and take) that took place while discussing the operating agreements they would follow was as important as the ultimate set of agreements.

As the manager in charge of this activity, you can facilitate the meeting by pointing out that for the team to function at a high level, people must be willing to be influenced by others and must be willing to influence in turn. You can also point out that a group of individuals who cannot influence and be influenced will find it difficult to coalesce into a high-performing team.

Excuse the repetition, but it is critical that you are clear that underlying the perspective and tools of the doing phase is the notion that managers manage *commitments* rather than activities or actions. If you are going to manage commitments, it is imperative that you have clear operating agreements in place as a standard, or base of understanding, from which you can fully support your people and make your assessments about productivity, innovation, and performance.

When you have agreed on your operating agreements, you and your team members must then hold each other accountable. No individual can be allowed to unilaterally change the agreement, but the team, agreeing as a whole, can change one or more guidelines at any time. This allows you to manage commitments. You do not have to convince anyone, argue with anyone, or yell at anyone.

At the same time, you also can't ignore it when people do not deliver or raise their hand. Meet with them briefly to find out what is going on (inquiry) by asking what they need in order to be able to keep the commitment they've made. You may have to find out what kind of support they require. When you listen to people's responses, you learn a lot. You may find out that they take on too much work or that they just can't say no or negotiate. They may not understand how important they are for the success of a given project. In some cases we're talking about self-centeredness versus individuals with a sense of community and thus responsibility toward their cohorts. We observe that some people live in the *I do work* mind-set, what we call a separated framework, rather than the *I do work for someone* mind-set, which is more of a connected framework. Some just don't get that people are connected and dependent on one another.

Perspective:
Frames of Reference

The following is an operating agreements document from a software development company showing how their commitments line up with the three cornerstones.

- We commit to continuously generate an accountability culture and use the Conversation Engine communication system.

- When we commit to certain goals/objectives we will treat those as top-priority and we will not change course on our own. (Alignment)

- We intend to support each other's dependencies within and outside the team, using negotiation when we are overloaded. (Integration)

- We agree to keep commitments with each other, including "raising our hand" if something goes wrong. (Accountability).

- We will clarify roles, responsibilities, and authority so people have clarity about their job.

- We have operating agreements in place and agree to hold each other accountable to our group determined operating agreements.

- We are committed to being on time, mentally present, ready to go for meetings.

Note that in the operating agreements between marketing and development above, everyone agreed to raise their hands. When you use the conversation engine's request–promise cycle that we showed you and you get a group commitment to raise hands, you have positioned everyone to increase productivity, reduce waste and unproductive conversations, and make things a lot easier on yourself as the leader. This is your key leverage point for building accountability and getting things done.

Now let's see how you can use this tool. We'll look at two situations:

Situation 1 (Prior to implementing the high-performance system and the *raise your hand* operating agreement):

Mary has agreed to send John, her boss, her completed report by Thursday at 4:00 p.m. On Thursday at 4:15 p.m., John notes that he has no report. At 5:00 p.m., he sees Mary in the hallway and says, "Mary, you didn't send the report you promised by 4:00 p.m. today."

"Oh, I got busy with three other projects," Mary responds.

"But you promised it," John reminds her.

Mary, with her voice going up several notches, repeats, "I told you—I got busy."

John is now wondering what to do. He is angry but knows that yelling in the office won't get him anywhere. Every time he has gotten angry, he not only has had to undo hard feelings but also ultimately hasn't gotten the result he wanted. He can't think of anything to do or say, so he stomps off to his office.

Notice that John has few moves left after confronting Mary. He can yell, try to convince her to apologize and provide the report, or sell her on the value of keeping her word—all of which Mary can easily ignore. Also, it puts John in a weak position, because he's responding very much in kind to her overt display of insubordination, responding on her level rather than displaying his leadership competence by rising above. Here's the key point: Remember that when you bring up a failed delivery with someone, that person will always find an excuse. It's human nature.

The authors have a theory that relying on excuses worked early in our lives; we got away with certain things if we had a good to great excuse, and that has carried over into our work lives. Key takeaway: we need to beat the excuse tendency in order to get accountability and the results we're after.

Situation 2 (Same situation with John and Mary, but *after* they have implemented the committed communication request–promise system and have in place the raise-your-hand operating agreement that Mary has committed to with her group):

It is now 5:00 p.m., and John sees Mary in the hallway. He asks her to step into his office for a moment then and says, "I didn't get the report you promised by 4:00 p.m. today."

Mary answers, "Oh, I got busy with three other projects."

John responds, "Okay, I understand … (he's ignoring the excuse) … and you promised to raise your hand and let me know if you wouldn't be able to do it. I didn't see an e-mail or get a phone message. Do you remember the operating agreements that we all committed to last week?"

Mary mumbles, "Oh yeah, I remember."

John continues, "Mary, this is not about whether you are a good or bad person. But in the accountability system we are using, we have all agreed to keep our commitments or inform the person if we can't deliver. You did not keep your promise. I'm asking you now if you agree to keep your commitments or to raise your hand to notify me in the future."

Here, Mary must answer yes or no. If she says no, you'll need to get your group together and have Mary explain why she is unwilling to keep the agreement to raise her hand. Be careful to simply explore what is going on here—do not lynch her.

Our Viewpoint: Leaders and managers are not charged with motivating anyone in the sense of selling someone on the value of doing his or her job. But they are charged with determining who will be accountable—or who will step up to being accountable— and then giving everyone a chance to prove that they intend to play the commitment game for the sake of the group and of delivering on their part in the agreement.

Are You Wondering How This Works Out?

After the marketing and development groups created operating agreements, they began to be more productive, wasting less energy on the needless conflict, arguments, and infighting that had been prevalent. Managers noted a gradual but persistent drop in these negative behaviors. While people did not immediately operate within all the agreements, over time they modified their behavior and began to align their actions with their stated intentions.

Their managers routinely brought up the agreements, talking in a light but persistent manner with those who were failing to keep their commitments until all were routinely following through on their own agreements. The development manager reported productivity was up by about 35 percent in only six months—as measured by compliance with the stated delivery dates of software iterations, the number of bug fixes by category, and the number of customer complaints by category as compared with his previous delivery measurements.

Summary

We have maintained that you can leverage the power granted you as a leader if you *manage commitments rather than activities or actions*. However, remember that if you are going to manage commitments, it is imperative that you have clear operating agreements in place as a standard, or base of understanding, from which you can fully support your people and make your assessments about productivity, innovation, and performance.

In our next chapter we continue with the *doing*, taking a look at the importance of roles, responsibilities, and authority.

CHAPTER 11

Roles, Responsibility, and Authority

Now that we've taken a look at the conversation engine and the importance of having operating agreements, it's time to explore our next tool.

In our work with various companies, we often run into interesting situations in which leaders, managers, and contributors working on various projects and tasks have become confused or are facing breakdowns. There are a number of factors we can address, but a key one, a foundational element, is that of defining roles, responsibilities, and authority. We claim that managers have unnecessary difficulties with production, partly because they do not have a clear understanding of the critical importance of defining roles, responsibilities, and authority. In our experience, managers typically think they fully understand these commonsense terms and have addressed them successfully. All too often, however, they have not taken the time to go over their reports' role(s), responsibilities, and authority so that all parties are aligned and in agreement. Notice that cornerstone alignment goes much deeper than just being focused on the same goal.

In this regard, Marvin Bower, in *McKinsey Quarterly*, wrote,

> In even the largest and best-managed companies, hundreds of organizational muddles take place every day. Throughout the economy, they add up to a staggering waste of our national resources.

Bower goes on to relate an incident regarding a golf game in which a friend asked him to join as a third. They talked about who would contact a fourth, but they did not indicate who would do the contacting.

It turns out that they had each invited another person, so they had five now signed up to play. Bower noted that the incident was embarrassing and could have been avoided by simply deciding who would make a contact. He adds, "All we had needed to do in our first telephone conversation was to follow one of the most fundamental principles of organization: decide who does what. In more technical terms, we should have fixed on one of us the responsibility for getting the fourth player and delegated the authority to do so."[1]

The Importance of Good Organization

Unfortunately, hundreds of organizational muddles of much greater consequence take place every day in even the largest and best-managed companies. The causes are often rooted in a failure to define who does what, who has what authority, and who reports to whom. The consequences of the resulting mix-ups and conflicts are duplication, wasted effort, delay, frustration, angry words, or pulling back and letting the other fellow do it. These countless mix-ups and conflicts throughout a company combine to bring about ineffective performance, needlessly high costs, a loss of competitive position, low morale, reduced profits, and lost opportunities to develop executives. Results like these throughout a company add up to a staggering waste of our national resources.

Mike, the CEO, of a company with forty-five retail outlets, had an executive vice president and VP of sales comprising his leadership team. While he was adamant about store managers having clear roles, responsibilities, and clear authority, for some reason he resisted this with his leadership team. The executive vice president and sales VP found, much to their chagrin, that they often got in each other's way on various projects and thoroughly confused the people who reported to them with their contradictory directions, project priorities, and decisions. When the CEO finally realized how dysfunctional his team was, he allowed us to help him clarify roles, responsibilities, and authority for each of his leadership team members. Needless to say, the team began to function more smoothly, and store leaders commented on "things working better."

Before we dive deeper into this, let's take a look at some research by the Gallup Organization regarding what they called *great workplaces.* In attempting to define a great workplace, the researchers decided that two criteria were central to their findings:

1. Employees were satisfied with their jobs.
2. The company was producing positive business outcomes.

These criteria led researchers to focus on four outcome variables: employee retention, customer satisfaction, productivity, and profitability.[2] They ranked the comments, with the number-one comment being "I know what is expected of me at work."

Gallup writes, "Expectations are the milestone against which we test our progress. Within the workplace, knowing what is expected can be viewed as the pathway that guides us toward achievement.

If expectations are not clear, we are hesitant, indecisive, and unsure of ourselves."[3]

Overlooking the critical importance of any employee being crystal clear regarding his or her role(s), responsibilities—and the authority granted to those roles—leads to breakdowns and waste. This may sound like a no- brainer, but we have never worked with a company, department, or team that had rigorously addressed the delegation process to our satisfaction. Confusion regarding any of these areas will result in needless conflict and a serious reduction of motivation leading to lowered productivity.

The Antidote

Begin by taking the time to ensure that your subordinates are clear about their roles, know what they have the responsibility to do in those roles, and understand the authority they have been granted. By clarifying their responsibilities and the specific authority you grant them to cover their position and accomplish their specific objectives, you will have taken a very positive step in your leadership or management competence. In addition, you will find that your direct reports will appreciate knowing exactly what is expected and how they can execute and win in the process. They will be clear about what they can decide on their own and which decisions and actions are not theirs to make without your participation.

Let's define these terms so that we are clear:

1. **Role:** Typically, the role is the job title. Let's take a fairly straightforward example, that of an administrative assistant who is stationed in the main lobby of a large company. Typically this person is the first point of contact for customers and vendors. Clearly defining a person's title and role provides a clear picture of where they should be directing their energy and where they should not be involved.

2. **Responsibilities:** Think of a position advertisement that defines what the position is, what the person's job includes, and what it excludes. In the role of administrative assistant stationed in the company's lobby, a person might be responsible for greeting people, checking to assure that guests are escorted into the building, and answering the phone when people call the company. On the other hand, for example, the administrative assistant is *not* responsible for personally handling various issues, complaints, or breakdowns that come up in the operation of the business.

3. **Authority:** The administrative assistant may have authority to make certain decisions that pertain to safety and/or security granted by your boss. Your reports need to know what authority (e.g., decision making, hiring/firing, budgeting, resource allocation, etc.) has been granted as part of their role and responsibilities. Serious breakdown results when people are not given proper authority yet are charged with the delivery of critical products. In our example of the administrative assistant, he or she may have the authority to allow certain people into the inner offices while excluding others.

It bears repeating that giving someone responsibility, having them make commitments, and then not being clear on their authority is a setup for failure, as you will see in the examples below:

A CFO called to tell us her boss had decided, on his own, to not renew a license for a financial program critical to her in producing on her commitments. She was distraught, as you might imagine, and did not know what to do. In this situation, the CEO had defined her role as CFO and made her overall responsibilities clear to her, but he never thought to discuss the authority granted for the position, including what decisions she could make. She felt undermined later on when he unilaterally made a decision that was, in her view, rightfully her call. When we presented her situation to her boss he realized how he had blocked her from successfully carrying out her responsibilities and reversed his decision.

In another situation, Jerry, a project leader, had been asked by his boss to take charge of an existing project team. Two weeks later, Jerry told his boss that Mike, a team member, was not doing his share of the work, not attending meetings, and had a bad attitude.

What authority does Jerry have to replace Mike? Can he fire him? Maybe he can't fire him because the boss holds that decision power, but possibly he could deselect Mike from the team. In this situation Jerry had not been granted the authority to fire or deselect. When Jerry's boss failed to respond to his requests to get Mike off his team, productivity was negatively impacted, and Jerry found himself demoralized and feeling undervalued by his boss. Jerry's boss was not open to coaching; thus, there was little Jerry could do to change the situation on this project. However, he demonstrated that learning had taken place when he later told us he would be sure to discuss authority issues when given new projects.

If you are beginning to see value in one of the first steps of positioning—clarifying roles, responsibilities, and authority—you may want to get started. The best way to gain competence is to jump right in, so choose a report and try the templates that follow. Feel free to do it awkwardly and make mistakes.

Let's take a look at the two worksheets that you can use immediately. The first is the leader's or manager's template, while the second is the direct report's copy. The process works best when you sit with your report and fill in the sections of the respective templates together. The process gives you an opportunity to discuss and clear up any confusion.

> Below you will see a sample of the leader's template that has been filled in for a production manager. You will also find a blank template at the end of this chapter as well as a template for your direct report to fill out.

Roles and Responsibilities Example: Production Manager

Responsibilities

- Responsible for establishing the direction, focus, and manufacturing department teams spanning multiple shifts.
- Responsible for quality on time and cost performance.

- Responsibility for the development and implementation of an organizational structure that supports production needs spanning multiple shifts.

- Responsible for recruiting, staffing, and training of skilled and semiskilled positions to support ongoing production needs in a high-growth environment.

- Responsible for ensuring appropriate skill level and ability for all positions.

Productivity Requests

What you as a manager are asking this person to do in what-by-when format?

1. Reduce labor/material cost/case to < S7 end of Q4

    - Deploy CT scanning

2. Reduce nonvalue added time in DAAD process to < 25% process time

    - Auto file transfer

3. Reduce rework/scrap to 0%—end of Q4

4. Reduce data distribution error rate to <1%—end of Q4

5. Keep spending at or below plan (assuming volume at plan)—ongoing

Performance Requests

This is what you, as a manager, are asking this person to do regarding *how* they manage.

John committed to the following:

1. Shift from heroic to manager-as-developer management style:

    1. Delegating: utilizing the committed communication process

    2. Tracking: use notebook to log all requests and promises

    3. Coaching: meet with each other, report two times per month using support and/or coaching system

    4. Operational agreements in place

2. Growing and developing people:

    1. All direct reports know and use a committed communication process in their interactions.

    2. All direct reports have clear written roles, responsibilities, and authority by end of the quarter.

    3. All direct reports have written commitments for delivery around those roles, responsibilities, and authority.

Authority and Communication Matrix

Activity	Owner	Approval	Collaborate
Inform			
Decisions that impact productivity (OT)	DIR	VP	
Decisions that impact on-time delivery	DIR	VP	
Decisions that impact quality	DIR	VP	
Functional Dept. Processes and Policies	VP	DIR	
Functional Dept. Budget	VP	DIR	
Functional Dept. Spending (within limit)	DIR	VP	

On the next pages you will find templates for the leader and direct report to fill in.

Templates

Leader's Worksheet

... for a direct report

Roles, Responsibilities, Authority, Requests (Commitments/Objectives), and Communication Expectations

Name of Report _____

Role (Title) _____

Responsibilities:

Broad areas responsible for covering ... like a job description.

List below:

1.

2.

3.

4.

5.

6.

Productivity Requests (Objectives): The *What* to Be Done

(What you, as manager, are asking this person to accomplish in what-by-when format.)

Ongoing Requests: What You Are Asking This Person to Do on a Regular Basis

1.

2.

3.

4.

5.

Quarterly or Special Projects:

1.

2.

3.

4.

5.

Productivity Commitments:

(In response to your productivity requests, your direct report also writes his or her commitments to producing in what-by-when format on the worksheet. These could be in the form of MBOs or commitments.)

1.

2.

3.

4.

5.

Performance Requests: How the Person Goes About Performing

These are requests related to how this person goes about producing. Does the person alienate people or win them over? These could include style, mood, and how relationships/dependencies are handled within and between groups. For example, are people being taken care of in the process of producing, or are work relationships being damaged? This could include situations such as working across functions, vendors, and companies to support others' dependencies. An example might be asking your report to take the company's communication class by the end of the next quarter (what by when).

These can also be areas for growth and development for top performers. As a stretch goal, you invite your report to check the executive management courses offered by Stanford University and get back to him within three weeks to see if he or she would like to enroll in one of them.

Performance Requests:

Document your requests below.

1.

2.

3.

4.

5.

Performance Commitments:

(In response to your performance requests, the direct report writes his or her commitments to you on his or her worksheet. Document what your report promised in what-by-when format below so you have a record.)

1.

2.

3.

4.

5.

Authority and Communication:

This section details the communication expectations and *authority* you have delegated to your report to carry out his or her commitments. The communication matrix lets your report know your expectations regarding updates (inform), when you would like to work with your report (collaborate), when you want to give the okay on something (approval), and when you have given your report ownership of a project (owner). This informs you and your report regarding what, when, and how you need to be contacted, reducing the need for your report to guess about what is wanted.

Authority & Communication Matrix:

Commitment/ Task	Owner	Approval	Collaborate	Inform

About Productivity and Performance

After defining and clarifying the overall role and the responsibilities you will be delegating, ask yourself what specifically you are requesting your report to get done. This typically takes the form of objectives for your report. These identify *what* is to be done. We've found it extremely useful to make a distinction between *what* is to be done (i.e., productivity) and *how* the person goes about producing (i.e., performance).

- Productivity is the *what* to be done.
- Performance is *how* productivity is carried out.

Productivity Commitments

In response to your productivity requests, your direct reports write their commitments to produce on their worksheets in the what-by-when format. These statements could be in the form of MBOs or commitments.

Performance Objectives

As noted above, these are requests from you regarding how this person goes about producing, including style, mood, and the ways relationships/dependencies are handled within and between groups. In this category you are determining whether people are being taken care of in the process of producing or are being damaged in some way that results in the work relationship being threatened. This might include things such as how your reports are interacting with others when working across functions, with vendors, or with other companies, as well as whether they are supportive of others' productivity needs (dependencies).

Performance Commitments

In response to your performance requests, your direct reports should write their commitments to you *on their worksheets.* (See the end of chapter for a direct report's worksheet.)

Authority and Communication Expectations

This section of the worksheet details the authority you have delegated and when and how you would like your reports to communicate with you. Communication expectations refers to how you want to maintain visibility for various projects and tasks. You may want to collaborate with your report, simply be kept informed, or maintain decision-making authority on certain elements of a given project. In our template, you will see the communication matrix, which you can easily use to clarify how you want to be informed of progress.

Action Assignment

Use the worksheet with at least one of your direct reports during the next week to set up roles, responsibilities, authority, and communication expectations. Be sure to document so that each of you has a copy of the template. This doesn't have to be perfect. Just do it, and you will see progress each time you go over the template with someone. Also, remember that the discussion that occurs naturally in and around the key areas between you and your report is crucial to your success as a leader and to the success of each of your direct reports.

Performance Commitments

(How people go about producing, interacting with, and supporting others)

Performance commitments are requests related to how reports go about producing, including style, mood, and the ways relationships/dependencies are handled within and between groups. For example, are people being taken care of in the process of producing or are work relationships being damaged? These interactions might include situations such as working across functions, vendors, companies, and so forth, to support others' dependencies.

Performance commitments can also be areas for growth, development, and stretch goals, as noted in your reports' annual appraisals.

In response to your performance requests as manager, if any, your reports should write their commitments in what-by-when format. An example might be a request that someone take the company's communication class and your report's response that she will have taken the course by the end of the next quarter (what by when). Or, as a stretch goal, you might ask a report to check the executive management courses offered by Stanford University and get back to you within three weeks to see if he would like to enroll in one of them.

Authority and Communication

This worksheet section details the communication expectations and *authority* delegated to reports to carry out their commitments. The communication matrix lets them know what you expect regarding updates (informing) and when you would like to work with them (collaborating). The matrix also gives them the authority to know when you want to give the okay on something (approval) and when they have been given ownership of a project (owner). This informs them and you about what, when, and how they need to communicate with you, reducing the need to guess about what is wanted. Subordinates also have needs when it comes to communication. Situations where problems arise, like Jerry's problem, can be avoided if it is made clear that he has the right to expect a timely response to such an issue when he has not been granted the authority to solve such a problem on his own.

Summary

In this chapter we have presented and discussed the importance of defining roles, responsibilities, and authority. Despite these terms being commonplace, we noted that leaders and managers have unnecessary difficulties with production, partly because they do not have a clear understanding of this foundational element critical to high-performance.

We recommended that the best way to gain competence is to jump right in clarifying roles, responsibilities, and authority using our templates. Feel free to do it awkwardly and make mistakes, but do it, as you will be pleased with the results.

Direct Report's Worksheet

Role, Responsibilities, Commitments, Authority, Communication

Name _____

(Title)_____

Role: Responsibilities:

Broad areas responsible for covering; similar to a job description.

List below:

1.

2.

3.

4.

5.

Productivity Requests (Objectives): The What Is to Be Done

Productivity Commitments:

Ongoing: (See attached sample of administrative/graphics person's ongoing and special commitments.)

1.

2.

3.

4.

5.

Quarterly or Special Commitments: (These include projects, initiatives, and so on. In response to your manager's productivity requests, write your commitments to producing in what-by-when format. These could be in the form of MBOs and/or commitments.)

1.

2.

3.

4.

5.

Performance Commitments:

(How you go about producing, interacting with, and supporting others.)

These are requests related to how you go about producing, including style, mood, and how relationships/dependencies are handled within and between groups. For example, are people being taken care of in the process of producing or are work relationships being damaged? These might include situations such as working across functions, vendors, companies, and so forth, to support others' dependencies.

Performance commitments can also be areas for growth, development, and stretch goals as noted in your annual appraisal.

In response to your manager's performance requests, if any, write your commitments in what-by-when format. An example might be your boss asking that you take the company's communication class and you respond that you will have taken the course by the end of the next quarter (what by when). Or, as a stretch goal, your boss asks you to check the executive management courses offered by Stanford University and get back to him within three weeks to see if you would like to enroll in one of them.

Performance Commitments:

1.

2.

3.

4.

5.

Authority and Communication:

This section details the communication expectations and authority you have been delegated to carry out your commitments. The communication matrix lets you know what your manager expects regarding updates (inform), when they would like to work with you (collaborate), when they want to give the okay on something (approval), and when they have given you ownership of a project (owner). This informs you and your manager about what, when, and how you need to communicate with them, reducing the need to guess about what is wanted.

Authority & Communication Matrix:

Commitment/ Task	Owner	Approval	Collaborate	Inform

CHAPTER 12

Tracking and Influencing

We've now covered the following three tools:

1. The conversation engine

2. Operating agreements

3. Roles, responsibilities, and authority

When any one of these three tools is overlooked or missing, the result has been costly in terms of leadership and management power: that is, effectiveness in getting things done. We've found that these tools fully support a team or unit maintaining alignment, integration (fully supporting each other), and accountability.

Let's now take a look at the critical importance of tracking and influencing as related to the three tools in action.

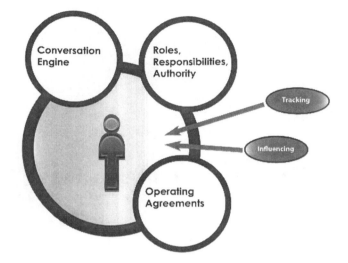

With regard to tracking, the former US Secretary of Defense Donald Rumsfeld has said, "What you measure improves." The military version is, "You get what you inspect, not what you expect."[1] In his book, *Rumsfeld's Rules*, he emphasized that it is not easy to decide what to measure, because the decision has made clear your top priorities and what you are not going to be doing.

The next tool, tracking and influencing, allows you to effectively inspect. You will be able to track promises/commitments, influence people as needed, and support your reports in dealing with breakdowns, issues, and opportunities. Also, you will keep track of commitments you have made.

Tracking Commitments and the Self-Management System

Tracking involves checking the progress made on commitments to you, the manager. The tracking process allows you to maintain visibility into various stages of projects you have assigned. Within small companies, this often can be accomplished through e-mail updates, telephone messages, or in-person conversations. The tracking tool and conversation helps determine how often you need to be updated on progress for various commitments, based on urgency and an assessment of the amount of support the accountable individual might require.

Managers need a self-management system (PDA or notebook) for keeping track of the myriad requests (delegations) they have made from day to day. They need to know when things are moving smoothly and when there are glitches. They need to know when performance is lagging behind agreed-upon timelines and when there is substandard performance. Lacking information, managers often fail to support their people, make important decisions or take other appropriate, timely action to keep projects and people on track.

When Tom Hayse, CEO of Electromatic, Inc., implemented our system, he sent the following strong message to all leaders and employees: "Every ETMer needs your own self-management system in which you will make, document, and manage commitments made to you by others your own. Additionally, you will need to document and manage commitments to your internal and external customers." A PDA or notebook was recommended, as leaders could carry it with them wherever they traveled in the course of their day.[2]

Tracking Assignment

For this exercise, secure a small spiral notebook or an electronic device you can carry around with you. As noted above, do not use your desktop computer, as you won't have it when you need to make a note or check some deliverable. Each day for the next week, log each request you make by noting

1. the person who has committed,
2. what you asked in what-by-when format, and
3. when he or she has committed to deliver it.

Review your notebook each day to see what has been done and what has been dropped. Also log promises you have made, and check those daily as well. Tracking will bring to the surface concerns that may point to potential and actual breakdowns. This is when top leaders use influencing conversations. Despite having this knowledge, some leaders continue to simply cope or ignore problems.

Influencing: Confronting and Supporting

As noted, tracking will surface issues and breakdowns. In order to manage effectively, consider that you absolutely must confront these issues and breakdowns rather than let things go and hope they will work themselves out. Having said that, one of the authors, Robert, could have started nonconfronters anonymous, but he saw the light, so to speak, and now can effectively deal with issues, even though he does not particularly enjoy the process. He's clear that procrastinating or avoiding issues negatively impacts his productivity, identity, and dignity and is a huge waste of energy.

Many managers are skilled at ignoring problems and breakdowns, finding ways to avoid confronting the issues that inevitably arise. When these reluctant managers do confront issues, they often escalate the differences between teams and among team members and miss opportunities to strengthen relationships. When leaders don't act to effectively resolve issues and breakdowns, they also miss the chance to keep projects on track and thus to develop the team's competence.

When the breakdowns that are part of life, especially a manager's life, occur, the opportunity for people to learn is at hand. Facing issues or confronting someone regarding a productivity or performance concern or breakdown is critical to high performance. In this context, the word *confront* means simply to bring something to someone's attention. It does not imply *an aggressive, hostile manner*. The intention is to get someone back on track and develop that person's competence.

The purpose of the conversation is to improve productivity or performance while building the relationship. The process encourages the direct report to learn and develop competencies to enhance productivity and innovation. The intention is for you, as manager, to stay on what we call *high ground* by managing the conversation in a manner that achieves your objectives while reducing fear, guilt, and confusion.

Bob Weyant says: "Effective leaders deal with issues and breakdowns by solving problems. Effective leaders, when they experience any problem, immediately address the issue. They perceive objectively first what the problem is and its causes, including their own behavior, and then what realistic options they have—they face reality."[3]

For some of us, however, this is a risky proposition, at least in certain situations. Let's see what we can do to increase our intention and competence in influencing.

Key Point

Breakdowns, while not desirable, are always opportunities to advance your leadership competence and improve your high-performance accountability system.

You can use every breakdown as an opportunity to deepen your people's understanding of the accountability system, while reinforcing and driving the implementation of the system. Now that you have a context for managing production, you can look forward to each chance to deepen the learning and foster people's use of the system. Rather than avoiding issues, you can now see them as opportunities: a new perspective. When we present this approach in companies, there are always people who challenge our notions. At first we worried about this, wondering, *What if we don't have a good response?* or *What if they make us look incompetent, or we lose control?* Then we began to see our trainees were providing us with an opportunity to deepen a point or reinforce a concept. Rather than being fearful, we began to welcome challenges. In a similar vein, you can begin to see those unwanted breakdowns as opportunities to further develop your culture of accountability.

The Influencing Conversation: Objectives

Refine your skill at confronting breakdowns and influencing others, focusing on several objectives:

a. Increase your managerial power and effectiveness by turning breakdowns and issues into opportunities. This will increase productivity and help you grow your people.

b. Avoid procrastination and effectively deal with productivity issues and/or performance issues.

c. Avoid argument and conflict.

d. Satisfactorily resolve the issue.

e. Help your reports increase their productivity and develop additional areas of competence in their roles.

f. Improve your working relationship with each person in the process.

g. Increase your dignity, energy, and enthusiasm for your work.

Brief Overview of the Process of Influencing

Step 1: Prepare for the Meeting

Regarding one of your direct reports, make a list of concerns, issues, or breakdowns you face in completing some project. Prior to meeting with the person, determine what you want to say and what request you want to make. Determine the results (typically new behavior) you intend as an outcome of this meeting.

Step 2: Conduct the Meeting

- Ask your report to listen to your concerns, and let him or her know there will be a chance to share his or her viewpoint in a moment.

- Share concerns, issues, breakdowns with the person.

- Help the person understand your point of view—offer your assessments and facts. Remember: your assessment is your opinion, and you may have some facts wrong, so be open to that possibility.

Step 3: Get Your Report's Response

- Get the person's thoughts and feeling regarding what you have shared. The key to success here is to listen to and understand the person rather than argue or try to convince the person that your view is the right viewpoint.
- Avoid arguing; ask clarifying questions.

Step 4: Make a Request(s)

- Remember requests need to be specific; include a date and time, and have clear conditions of satisfaction attached.

Step 5: Get the Person's Response to Each Request

- Remember that there are only four responses: yes, no, negotiate, or make a counteroffer. Commit to provide an answer for a specific date and time.

Step 6: Support the Person's Willingness to Work on Changing Behavior

- If possible, acknowledge the person's willingness to participate in the conversation and to work on new behavior.

Step 7: Hold Follow-Up Meeting

- Remind person of any commitments from the previous meeting.
- Check progress with each request, and if possible acknowledge person for improvement.

When someone's behavior is a concern to you—whether you are facing a productivity issue or a performance issue (behavioral issue), such as how the person goes about doing the work—you will able to track promises or commitments, influence people as needed, and support them in dealing with their breakdowns, issues, and opportunities. Working within the context of the three cornerstones and using the tools we've shared so far, you are ready to increase productivity.

Summary

With the previous tools of doing system in place and backed by your boss, you are set to blast by any *hold backs* to dealing with daily issues. You will be increasing your managerial power (effectiveness) by tracking and dealing with breakdowns and issues that need to be addressed in a timely fashion. We have seen an employee facing almost certain termination transform himself into a worker willing to change, collaborate, and successfully produce as a result of his manager using this system.

But wait, there is an invisible enemy lurking that might derail your efforts. We'll discuss this enemy in the next chapter.

For a detailed discussion of this process with an example, please see the Performance Conversation in chapter 7 from *Boss Talk*.

CHAPTER 13

Sponsorship Support:
The Power Cord

And now, a *warning*!

Bringing in a high-performance accountability system such as more, better, different will trigger resistance. This is normal, but some people will go way beyond the normal resistance level in their attempts to neutralize your new initiative. Some may be threatened by, disagree with, or have other priorities they prefer over your initiative. Sabotage may also enter the picture. It requires taking the initiative on your part to manage up the organization to get support and muster against resistance. Think of sponsorship— being backed and supported—as a positioning tool that will optimize your chances of succeeding with your change project. We think of it as your personal power cord.

As you work your way through the chapter you may also see what is required to fully support (sponsor) a report of yours who is driving a key project or initiative and therefore needs your backing.

Charan and Bossidy describe the dilemma faced by executives when potentially helpful initiatives fail. Typically, the failure is a result of resistance from direct reports and managers in the organization who, feeling that this too shall pass, pay little attention and wait for the idea to wither and die on the vine. The result is wasted time, money, and energy and a loss of credibility to leaders who frequently don't recognize the failure as a personal adjustment.

Charan and Bossidy go on to suggest, "The leader's personal involvement and commitment are necessary to overcome any passive (or in many cases active) resistance. The leader has to not only announce the initiative or project, but to define it clearly and define its importance to the organization. She can't do this unless she understands how it will work and what it really means in terms of benefit."[1]

Randall L. Englund, an expert in project management and sponsorship, seconds Charan and Bossidy's conclusion and adds, "This is a powerful statement, replete with many provocative elements. The one element I would like to highlight is *understanding*.

No executives, facing severe time and attention demands, will provide their support to initiatives they do not understand."[2] Therefore, it is of paramount importance to ensure that your potential sponsor understands the more, better, different *system*, its purpose, its fundamental principles, practical applications, and benefits.

Randy continues, "People are smart—they simply watch what their boss and their boss's boss do, not just what they espouse. If executives provide casual support to the change effort, that treatment will instantly be translated by others to mean this initiative can be ignored as *idea du jour.*"[3] Why should we expect people to commit to something that leaders appear reluctant to back themselves? People have all too many things to do already, so ignoring a project or initiative, when possible, is fully understandable. Randy offers *The Complete Project Manager* (2012), plus an accompanying *Toolkit*, as an organic metaphor for tapping all necessary disciplines that create environments for successful projects.

Consider that for a sustainable implementation and the desired results to occur, an active and dedicated sponsor is a necessary element. Maybe you already have a sponsor, possibly a CEO who has declared a change initiative and is clearly backing all efforts.

On the other hand, you may be driving a new project or be part of a change initiative that is running into resistance. You might be wondering how you can get things done given all the competing commitments people have. Our first question is, do you have a sponsor, and do you know what that actually means regarding desired behaviors your sponsor needs to exhibit?

Key Points:

1. Think of your sponsor as your power cord and *resistance reducer*.

2. When someone you report to requests or assigns a project or change initiative, you have a right to expect full support from that person. Strongly consider using the checklist we provide below to determine whether you *do* have that person's full support.

3. If possible, avoid committing until you are sure you have a sponsor. This action is necessary in order to avoid being set up for failure.

4. Ensure the sponsor understands and is willing to sustain support throughout the project life cycle.

Sponsorship Behaviors

Now let's take a look at the behaviors you want from your potential sponsor. The following are offered in Randy Englund's top-selling book *Project Sponsorship: Achieving Management Commitment for Project Success, 2nd Edition* (2015). Here's what to look for in your sponsor; he or she

- understands the big picture, why your project is so important to the company, and how the project links to strategic goals;
- actively develops and manages relationships;
- makes timely decisions;
- helps you deal with politics throughout project implementation;
- is clear about priorities that support focus on your project;
- can provide rapid and decisive resolution of conflicts, participating in an escalation process when needed;
- clarifies solutions to be delivered and the impact on internal and external customers;
- aids in resource allocation; and
- identifies areas of possible resistance across the organization.

How to Go About Securing Executive Sponsorship

1. Locate your sponsor and request a meeting.

2. Hold an interview in the executive's office.

    a. In order to receive candid feedback, it is critical that the executive feel comfortable. By holding the interview in his or her office, you have the opportunity to learn more about him or her based on furniture, pictures, etc. Something in this environment will provide an icebreaker if you need one.

        i. Consider having a note taker or request permission to record the meeting.

        ii. Share what you have committed to deliver and the benefits to the company; focus on features, benefits, and advantages.

        iii. Share your sense of the issues and current breakdowns, possibly as a review of previous successes and failures.

        iv. Get your executive's thoughts and opinions, and determine whether she or he sees the need for the project and cost of failed delivery; elicit a vision statement.

v. Provide a basic training or short briefing on the accountability system.

vi. Get the executive's thoughts on a definition of success, "yeah buts," and ideas, and then seek his or her advice for implementation.

vii. Request the executive's backing as a sponsor and get her or his response; an explicit commitment is the preferred response.

viii. Ask what, when, and how your sponsor prefers to communicate throughout the project.

Debriefing Checklist (following the meeting and ongoing)

Sponsorship

i. Has my sponsor or senior leader committed to a guiding vision of where this high-performance system can take the unit or company?

ii. Have we provided our potential sponsor(s) with an overview or brief training to ensure they understand the purpose, fundamentals, and benefits of the Get in the Game Leadership system?

iii. Have we ensured that our sponsor's voice is continually heard in the implementation by updating and ensuring involvement in the process?

iv. Does our executive sponsor deliver consistent messages at frequent intervals regarding the change initiative we are driving, including at project start-up and milestone events?

v. Does implementation impact any results the executive has committed to deliver? Does he or she have responsibility for meeting some specific targets this productivity process will address? How will the sponsor be measured?

vi. Is there evidence that in the ongoing management of the organization, our executive sponsor is actively modeling the behaviors the change initiative teaches?

vii. Will the sponsor passionately pursue achievement of benefits the project is chartered to produce?

Summary

We promise you will face some resistance bringing the productivity system we've been describing into your culture. While we noted this earlier, please strongly consider that for sustainable implementation and results to occur, an active and dedicated sponsor is a necessary element for project success. If you have a sponsor already, you may want to review our criteria and expectations to see if your sponsor is up to the challenge of supporting you. If no sponsor is on the horizon, make it a top priority to establish one … or make preparations to fail.

CHAPTER 14

Taking Care of Your People and Yourself

Asked to identity a manager's most important job when working with others, executives and managers typically suggest productivity, make a profit, or style. Certainly these are credible responses. After we get their answers, we have them think about and make some notes about their favorite job or position prior to becoming a manager and why they are listing that particular job. You could do that for yourself right now if you would like.

Invariably, participants come up with some version that always has as its theme the notion of having had a *great experience* that included some or all the following:

- My boss and associates were very supportive of my work.

- My boss and others listened to each other's point of view.

- People helped me deal with things and continually learn.

- My boss asked me what I personally wanted to achieve and where I saw myself in a few years.

- Most everyone recognized good work and said something.

- If someone got upset with me, my boss or someone would make sure things worked out for the person and for me. I liked that.

While these, of course, are not all-inclusive, they point to the boss having created a great experience for his or her people.

Consider that a manager's most important job is to create a supportive environment. We could have said production is the most important part of the job; however, that viewpoint is shortsighted, as people quickly burn out and look to jump ship or change careers when they are not feeling cared about. Experienced managers tell us that taking care of their people and building trust are essential, not optional. In our workshops, they list the following as central to long-term success:

- providing a supportive environment
- taking care of their people's work identity
- helping them to continually learn and add value
- supporting them with their career intentions

The high-performance system we've discussed is designed to increase the rigor of productivity interactions for the sake of increasing accountability and productivity. As you may have surmised, people can become anxious in the face of change and at times can feel damaged. The process can trigger defensive reactions. It's common for people to become hurt or upset and nonparticipative when confronted with poor performance. What is needed is the manager's intention to be supportive rather than harsh or demeaning. They need effective conversational tools to help them carry out that intention.

Jack Mitchell, CEO of Mitchells-Richards-Marsh, three of the most successful clothing stores in the business, wrote a book entitled *Hug Your People ... The Proven Way To Hire, Inspire, and Recognize Your Employees and Achieve Remarkable Results*. His main claim is that everyone wants to be appreciated. He adds that, when it comes to cultures, "It's how you treat one another" that really counts. Regarding hugs, he notes that more often than not it's a metaphor for what we do.[1]

When we talk about taking care of your people we're not suggesting that a manager's job is to go around giving people great big hugs. Rather, our notion is that taking care of yourself and others actually is a function of "the ways things are around here" or culture. In our experience the key to a positive, productive culture starts with mutual respect.

While certainly there are many factors one could include, we've focused on a few that are pertinent to high-performance productivity. These include but are not limited to

- reducing slippage and lack of accountability;
- increasing mutual respect by increasing the effectiveness of cooperation, collaboration, and coordination of action between associates;
- acknowledging accomplishment and celebrating key milestone delivery on projects;
- understanding and taking care of other's identities; and
- style considerations: aggressive, passive, assertive.

As noted earlier, a slippage environment creates upsets, conflict, and loss of energy, because people can't get—or are not sure about getting—what they need to deliver on their promises. We have noted the dangers of a slippage culture, in which people simply do what they choose and ignore what they don't get around to doing. Sometimes these people fail to notify associates that they will not be delivering on their promises, thereby creating surprises and reducing trust. In such cultures, work relations are damaged, and future work is jeopardized. People have shared with us how frustrated they were while attempting to get things done in this type of work culture.

Our experience suggests there is no evidence that any corporate start-up ever actively designed a slippage culture. There is no malevolence working here. No, it is clear that this is the result of a drift. Groups of well-intentioned, highly educated people have drifted into this insidious mode we've called slippage.

An accountability environment, on the other hand, paves the road to productivity and innovation when people are getting what they need from others to produce. In this environment, people make and keep promises to deliver and, if necessary, let their internal customers (associates) know when they are having problems delivering. *They take care of each other in this manner.*

Any activity that requires interaction with others demands skillful managing of myriad conversations. Competence in cooperation, coordination of action, and collaboration are the keys to successful operations management in any industry and to the satisfaction level achieved by the manager and each contributor.

What we have learned from managers is the basis for our claim that better interactions play a major role in sustained productivity, innovation, and well-being.

We, of course, are advocating the development of an accountability culture.

Accountability allows you to

- develop an aligned, collaborative team that pulls together;
- increase commitment to goals and objectives;
- effectively support and nurture your people as they produce their products and services; and
- increase your ability to troubleshoot problems and breakdowns and quickly get back on track.

As managers become better observers of the conversations they are having daily, they are able to make assessments about the efficacy of those conversations and, when necessary, make appropriate changes.

Our intention has been to bring a new awareness to the largely invisible yet critical process by which things get done—and to examine and bring to light the system underlying the actions that take place. That is, we have explored how people get things done by talking with each other, writing to one another, and making requests, promises, and offers.

Our theme, if you will, has been the power of collaboration, the ability to influence and be influenced in every area of work.

People who can influence and be influenced, in our experience, have a sense of mutual respect.

Clichés abound when it comes to teamwork and synergy, yet we find good management ultimately comes down to the simple notion of mutual influence. Without mutual influence, you can still coordinate action. For example, we know that there are command structures in which people can and do coordinate actions masterfully. They don't often think together, but they respond to orders, thus effectively carrying out one person's thinking and actions.

Collaboration, however, is a higher order of interacting that calls for the full participation of each person. When you are collaborating, you are fully engaged, thinking with the other person or persons in what we call a dance. The dance is one of listening, speaking, and sharing of ideas, intentions, and directions. In the process, ideas get shaped and reshaped. In the best cases there is a camaraderie that develops that supports thinking, action, and caring under stressful conditions. There is no credit given or asked for in this process; rather, it simply happens—and results come from the interaction of the participants.

Human beings are complex. Dealing with the variety of situations that will arise as you attempt to produce through others' efforts and manage situations where there is simply too much to do is not a simple matter. Building the accountability culture, understanding identity and the reactions it causes, managing moods and emotions, assessing trust, and building relationships while you deal with conflicts are all skills that enhance your ability to coordinate action and collaborate in highly interdependent environments.

CHAPTER 15

Tying Up the Package

We began this book with a promise that we would offer you a proven leadership system you could implement to generate a highly productive interaction dynamic. This dynamic changes the way people interact with other individuals, groups, or departments, and will allow you to accomplish more consistently and reliably the work you need to get done. While we authors get pumped up about having a phenomenal system, we realize that a key element here is the opportunity to instill a more effective *dynamic* into the human interactions that make up your business.

In this regard our client, Tracy Newquist, President, noted, "To me, it seems that what you are suggesting with MBD is that it is more of a shift in the dynamic in how we interact with and manage others. Implementing MBD, whether it is how we interact with clients or internally with managers and staff, is more a shift in philosophy, perspective and approach. Sure, the tools you provide have a 'system' to their implementation, but adopting MBD as a methodology actually results in a shift in the dynamic of how we lead. The dynamic that we have seen develop around our MBD system has enhanced relationships, improved productivity, and created a more dynamic, satisfying work environment."[1]

As a way to help you generate this new dynamic, we have focused on our MBD system and its application. Early on we issued a challenge saying that if we were betting men, we'd wager that you do not have a complete productivity system with complementary practices that support your transformation of high-level concepts and goals into great results. To close this gap, we've shared our perspective, positioning tools, and conversational tools—all designed to help leaders and managers get things done. Strategically, we've targeted how managers can consistently and successfully complete projects they have developed and documented. This system works because of the complementary nature of its elements and the way that perspective, positioning tools, and conversational tools are networked together.

Our system began with your foundation for success, which is comprised of

1. determining your present situation—your now—and identifying both opportunities and weak points for improvement;

2. planning a strategy that leads to actionable projects intended to produce desired outcomes—your future; and

3. getting those projects done—the doing, which creates a new now.

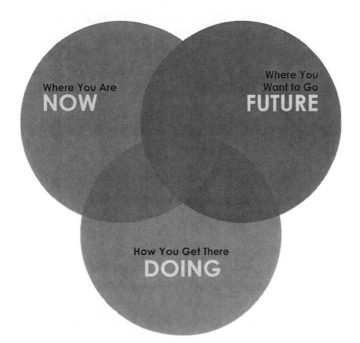

Diving deeper into these key elements, we offered perspective, positioning tools, and interaction tools to help you move smoothly from the future into the doing.

The Framework of Commitment Culture

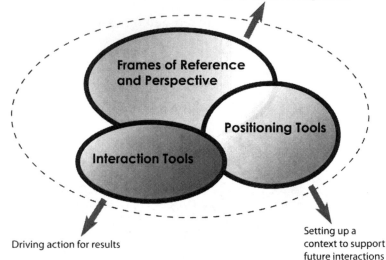

Leadership and management
viewpoint optimizing success

Frames of Reference
and Perspective

Positioning Tools

Interaction Tools

Driving action for results

Setting up a
context to support
future interactions

Frame of Reference and Perspective

As noted, your perspective or viewpoint is the lens, model, or paradigm you work from. Without your realizing it, your viewpoint is the source of your thoughts, behavior, and practices for managing. Given this century's dramatic global changes, however, your viewpoint—shaped by education, theory, and what worked in management in the past—may no longer be effective. This situation is compounded by the lack of new models designed or offered to help you get things done in this changed world of work.

We suggested that what you need is a different leadership and management perspective that changes how you look at and think about what an organization is. We contrasted the three basic models of organizations: hierarchical power, management by process, and managing by commitment. We explained that in the third model, business is not viewed through the lens of power or process but rather is seen as a network of promises people make to one another. The advantage of this approach is that it lends itself to moment-to-moment, on-the-fly situations and conversations that cannot be standardized, including the discussion of new strategies, ways to address breakdowns, and methods for dealing with creative opportunities.

Positioning Tools

Positioning is a way to optimize your odds of accomplishing intended goals by setting up a context for all future interactions. Positioning needs to happen before you roll up your sleeves and go to work on any new ideas or projects.

Let's take a look at the game of chess for a moment. Chess is about positioning, thinking ahead about what moves you need to make prior to delivering that wonderful declaration: checkmate. People we've worked with often don't fully understand the necessity of positioning in today's work environment. That is, they don't know how to set up their objectives/commitments in a context that will ensure support for their successful execution. Positioning tools help you bridge this gap and build the support you need to achieve your objectives.

Interaction Tools

A key point of view for us is that everything happens in communication with others. At work, leaders are interacting with others all day long, for better or for worse. We maintain that these leaders, in order to navigate their terrain once they understand the new perspective and the role of positioning, will need specific conversational tools not taught in their traditional training.

We want to pause here to strongly reiterate that you must have a proven leadership system, ours or someone else's, that you refer to in times of stress, breakdown, or opportunity. Our system, we maintain, is a proven one, with scores of clients to back up that claim. We know from experience that once we instill our system into a group, a team, or an entire company, the results are breathtaking.

Planning the Journey: Some Last Words

Often the key components of a managerial system are simply missing, out of order, or plain wrong, which leads to less-than-optimal results. Our goal in these pages is to offer a solution that avoids these pitfalls. Now that you have read about our system, you have an opportunity to become aware of your own leadership and management system, or lack of same, and to assess whether it is serving you in today's work world. Then, if you desire and see the need, you can consciously design your productivity system using the proven perspective, positioning notions, and conversation tools that we have presented.

Our central message to you is that the key to a leader's and organization's success is found in focusing on the lowly project and using a proven system for getting projects done, shown below, to effectively and consistently drive each project to completion.

The Elements in Action

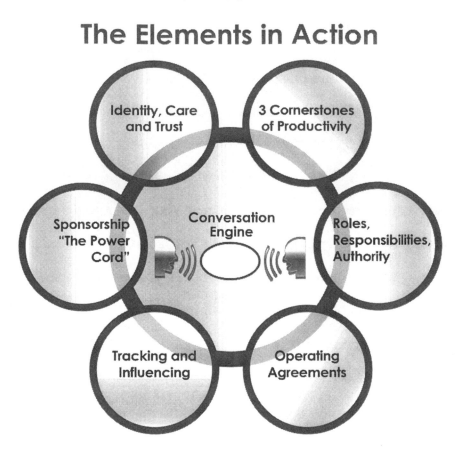

With this in mind, we've shared a system of complementary management practices as a way to instill in you a process that will dramatically increase your productivity through the efforts of others.

We have shared one pathway you can follow to put such a system in place, one that weaves complementary skills, tools, practices, operating agreements, and interactions into a shared fabric of processes and behaviors. This system offers a map to identifying—specifically—what needs to grow more, work better, and be replaced with something different. And it provides the tools and processes that will enable you to plan the journey and ultimately shape—and realize—your company's, and your own, future potential.

For owners of businesses, our intention is to increase your profitability and satisfaction. For leaders working inside organizations, our purpose is to help you increase your productivity, *up* your perceived value to the organization, elevate your *promotion potential*, and increase your earnings. Your increased worth, stemming from your ability to effectively deal with producing in a rapidly changing world that continually demands more of you while providing less, will be noticed. The great news is that people just like you have become effective and successful using this system and these processes.

To get started, determine whether you need to begin with your now situation or, if you are clear about that, check whether you have goals that are documented in project format in the future section. If not, jump in there, but if projects are documented to your satisfaction, you can go right to the doing. We recommend you go to www.lauridsenreinhardtgroup .com and view the conversation engine as a way of preparing yourself to get full value from the doing section. The conversation engine process takes practice and some patience, but you will find it is the heart of productivity in those situations where you are dependent on others to carry out various tasks.

We wish you all the very best in your leadership career, and we are available to support you as needed.

NOTES

Introduction

1   Morgan et al., *Executing Your Strategy* (Harvard Business School Press, 2007), 4–6.

Chapter 1

1   Steve Jobs, as quoted on www.Goodread.com from Apple Worldwide Developers' Conference, 1997.

2   Jodi Picoult, *Nineteen Minutes* (Atria Books, 2007).

3   Jack Kornfield, *A Path with Heart: A Guide Through the Perils and Promises of Spiritual Life* (Bantam Books, 1993).

Chapter 3

1   Dan Sullivan, *The Strategic Goal Tracker* (Canada: Strategic Coach, Inc.), 4.

Chapter 6

1   Andre Young, "Advanced CFO Solutions," blog post, 2007.

2   David Rock, *Quiet Leadership: Six Steps to Transforming Performance at Work* (New York: Harper Collins, 2010).

3   Based on the work of Donald Sull as quoted in Jeremy Dann, "Donald Sull: Manage by Commitments, Not Hierarchies," *Moneywatch* (March 4, 2009).

Chapter 7

1   Michael Paczan, personal correspondence.

Chapter 9

1   John Assaraf and Murray Smith, *The Answer* (California: Atria Books-Simon and Shuster, 2008), Kindle location 706-10.

2   For more information on the role of conversation in a committed context see the white paper *Creating Positive Relationships through Effective Interactions* at www.lauridsenreinhardtgroup.com.

3   Chauncey Bell, personal conversation, 2009.

Chapter 11

1   Marvin Bower, "The Online Journal of McKinsey & Company" (excerpt from Marvin Bower, *The Will to Manage*, 1966).

2   "What Makes a Great Workplace," *Gallup Management Journal*, April 2008.

3   Ibid.

Chapter 12

1 Donald Rumsfeld, *Rumsfelds' Rules: Leadership Lessons in Leadership, Politics, War and Life* (Massachusetts: Broadside Books, 2013).

2 Tom Hayse, CEO of ETM, Inc., personal communication, March 21, 2002.

3 Robert Weyant, *Confronting Without Guilt or Conflict* (Seattle, Washington: Brassy Publishing, 1994).

Chapter 13

1 Larry Bossidy and Ram Charan, *Execution: The Discipline of Getting Things Done,* Crown Business, June 4, 2002.

2 Randy Englund and Alfonso Bucero, *Project Sponsorship* (San Francisco: Jossey-Bass, 2006).

3 Ibid.

Chapter 14

1 Jack Mitchell, *Hug Your People: The Proven Way to Hire, Inspire, and Recognize Your Employees and Achieve Remarkable Results* (New York: Hyperion, 2008).

Chapter 15

1 Tracy Newquist, personal communication, May 21, 2016.

INDEX

N

negotiation (It's a Good Thing), as phase of conversations, 122, 126–132
Newquist, Tracy, 215
now
exercise for taking inventory of, 19–21
as one of three key elements of system, xxxiii, 18, 94, 217
present as designated as, 95–96

O

on-the-job training (OJT), 141
operating agreements, 139–155, 186, 222
operating agreements document, example of, 150
operating agreements worksheet, 146
organization, importance of good organization, 159–161
outcomes, increasing control over intended outcomes, xxxii–xxxvi

P

passion and motivation, 27, 28–29
past, as one of three common distinctions, 95
pathway conversation, finding of, 41, 44
Pathway Projects (worksheet), 52, 53
pathways
development of, 41–45
to projects, 47–55
performance (Getting to the Action), as phase of conversations, 122, 132–133
persistence, importance of, 62

planning, as first step in taking action and getting results, 107
positioning tools, 197, 216, 217, 218, 219–220
power cord, sponsorship support as, 197, 200
prepare, as one of four components of interactions, 118, 121
present, as one of three common distinctions, 95–96
productivity breakdowns, 58
productivity system
assessing current system, 3
conscious design of, 61
importance of, 12, 62
key elements of, xxxiii–xxxiv
lack of, 59
profitability, as standard of effectiveness, 109
project development process, as rubber meeting the road, 49
Project Sponsorship: Achieving Management Commitment for Project Success (Englund), 200
projects
doing/executing of, 57–69
pathways to, 47–55
talking about, 42
promotion potential, 223
purpose, 27, 28, 29

Q

questions to prime the pump
level 1 (executives), 22–24
level 2 (business owners), 24–26
Quiet Leadership (Rock), 66

R

raise your hand operating agreement, 151, 153
real work, 10, 11
receive customer feedback, as phase of conversations, 122, 133
Reinhardt, Carl H., xxx–xxxi, 10, 13–14, 97
request (I'm Asking), as phase of conversations, 122, 123–126
request–promise system, 152–153
resistance, 143, 197, 198, 200, 201
resources, section of Pathway Projects (worksheet), 54
respectful communication, 113
responsibilities, use of term, 162
responsiveness, as standard of effectiveness, 108
reward, 27, 28, 29
right-now periods of time/right-now items, 96, 97, 98
Rock, David, 66
role, use of term, 162
roles, responsibilities, authority, defining of, 157–184, 222
roles and responsibilities (production manager), tracking and influencing as related to, 186
rubber meeting the road, 49, 57
rules of the game, 139, 140. *See also* operating agreements
Rumsfeld, Donald, 185
Rumsfeld's Rules (Rumsfeld), 186

S

sabotage, 197
self-management system, 187
separate: me, as frame of reference, 149
slippage, 128, 210–211

sponsorship support, as element in action, 197–205, 222
status quo, leadership and, xxii
The Strategic Goal Tracker (Sullivan), 38
strategy execution, 57
success, key factors in, 55, 208, 221
Sull, Donald, 66
Sullivan, Dan, 38
sweet spot, 29

T

taking care of each other, xxxvi, 116, 208, 209, 210, 211
thinking together, 129
three-circle process, xxxiii–xxxiv. *See also* doing; future; more, better, and different (MBD); now
time and energy, required for thinking of something new as compared to doing it, 8, 9–10
Toolkit (Englund), 199
too-much-to-do phenomenon, 73
tracking
defined, 187
as element in action, 222
exercise, 188–189
importance of, 185–187

W

wants and desires, 4
webinar, 116
website, www.lauridsenreinhardtgroup.com, 116, 146, 223
Weyant, Bob, 190–191
what-by-when format/statement, 36, 37, 50, 54, 68, 117–118, 125, 166
work, interpretation of, 109–110
working in the business, as compared to working on the business, 3–4, 5, 7, 8, 10–11

worksheets
  direct report's copy, 165, 180–184
  Goal Pathway Planner
    (worksheet), 44
  leader's/manager's template, 165,
    168–179
  MBD worksheet, 36, 37

operating agreements
  worksheet, 146
Pathway Projects (worksheet),
  52, 53

Y

Young, Andre, 62

Open Book Editions
A Berrett-Koehler Partner

Open Book Editions is a joint venture between Berrett-Koehler Publishers and Author Solutions, the market leader in self-publishing. There are many more aspiring authors who share Berrett-Koehler's mission than we can sustainably publish. To serve these authors, Open Book Editions offers a comprehensive self-publishing opportunity.

A Shared Mission

Open Book Editions welcomes authors who share the Berrett-Koehler mission—Creating a World That Works for All. We believe that to truly create a better world, action is needed at all levels—individual, organizational, and societal. At the individual level, our publications help people align their lives with their values and with their aspirations for a better world. At the organizational level, we promote progressive leadership and management practices, socially responsible approaches to business, and humane and effective organizations. At the societal level, we publish content that advances social and economic justice, shared prosperity, sustainability, and new solutions to national and global issues.

Open Book Editions represents a new way to further the BK mission and expand our community. We look forward to helping more authors challenge conventional thinking, introduce new ideas, and foster positive change.

For more information, see the Open Book Editions website:
http://www.iuniverse.com/Packages/OpenBookEditions.aspx

Join the BK Community! See exclusive author videos, join discussion groups, find out about upcoming events, read author blogs, and much more! http://bkcommunity.com/

CPSIA information can be obtained
at www.ICGtesting.com
Printed in the USA
LVOW11*0223100417

530215LV00001B/5/P